School Lea... through the Seasons

M000111941

This book offers key tools and tactics that help school leaders navigate the complex and busy work of improving a school, allowing them to maintain success during the full calendar year. Through practical guidance and "Have to Do" strategies, *School Leadership through the Seasons* breaks down the challenges of leading a school into manageable steps that align with the seasons of the year. After reading this book, you'll be able to: implement school improvement processes at high levels, build a culture and climate that promotes safety and learning, and respond to student and staff needs. Full of concrete examples and practical strategies, this book provides focus and direction to ensure your school grows and flourishes for all 365 days of the year, allowing you to transform ideas into action.

Ann T. Mausbach is Assistant Professor for Educational Leadership at Creighton University and formerly held positions as an assistant superintendent for curriculum and instruction, coordinator of staff development, director of curriculum, and director of elementary education.

Kimberly Morrison is the principal of an urban middle school located in the Midwest and has been in elementary and district administration for over fifteen years.

Other Eye On Education Books
Available from Routledge
(www.routledge.com/eyeoneducation)

Distributed Leadership in Schools: A Practical Guide for Learning and Improvement
John A. DeFlaminis, Mustafa Abdul-Jabbar, and Eric Yoak

Principalship A to Z, Second Edition
Ronald Williamson and Barbara R. Blackburn

Leading Learning for Digital Natives: Combining Data and Technology in the Classroom
Rebecca J. Blink

Strategies for Developing and Supporting School Leaders: Stepping Stones to Great Leadership
Karen L. Sanzo

Crafting the Feedback Teachers Need and Deserve: A Guide for Leaders
Thomas Van Soelen

Becoming a Social Justice Leader: Using Head, Heart, and Hands to Dismantle Oppression
Phil Hunsberger, Billie Mayo, and Anthony Neal

Formative Assessment Leadership: Identify, Plan, Apply, Assess, Refine
Karen L. Sanzo, Steve Myran, and John Caggiano

The Leader's Guide to Working with Underperforming Teachers: Overcoming Marginal Teaching and Getting Results
Sally Zepeda

Five Critical Leadership Practices: The Secret to High-Performing Schools
Ruth C. Ash and Pat H. Hodge

Mentoring is a Verb: Strategies for Improving College and Career Readiness
Russ Olwell

How to Make Data Work: A Guide for Educational Leaders
Jenny Grant Rankin

Hiring the Best Staff for Your School: How to Use Narrative to Improve Your Recruiting Process
Rick Jetter

Get Organized! Time Management for School Leaders, Second Edition
Frank Buck

School Leadership through the Seasons

A Guide to Staying Focused and Getting Results All Year

Ann T. Mausbach and
Kimberly Morrison

Routledge
Taylor & Francis Group

NEW YORK AND LONDON

First published 2016
by Routledge
711 Third Avenue, New York, NY 10017

and by Routledge
2 Park Square, Milton Park, Abingdon, Oxon, OX14 4RN

Routledge is an imprint of the Taylor & Francis Group, an informa business

© 2016 Taylor & Francis

The right of Ann T. Mausbach and Kimberly Morrison to be identified
as authors of this work has been asserted by them in accordance with
sections 77 and 78 of the Copyright, Designs and Patents Act 1988.

All rights reserved. No part of this book may be reprinted or
reproduced or utilised in any form or by any electronic, mechanical,
or other means, now known or hereafter invented, including
photocopying and recording, or in any information storage or retrieval
system, without permission in writing from the publishers.

Trademark notice: Product or corporate names may be trademarks
or registered trademarks, and are used only for identification and
explanation without intent to infringe.

Library of Congress Cataloging in Publication Data
Names: Mausbach, Ann T., author. | Morrison, Kimberly, author.
Title: School leadership through the seasons : a guide to staying
focused and getting results all year / Ann T. Mausbach and
Kimberly Morrison.
Description: New York, NY : Routledge, 2016. | Includes
bibliographical references.
Identifiers: LCCN 2015044004| ISBN 9781138998308 (hardback) |
ISBN 9781138998315 (pbk.) | ISBN a9781315658759 (ebook)
Subjects: LCSH: Educational leadership. | School improvement
programs. | School management and organization.
Classification: LCC LB2805 .M294 2016 | DDC 371.2—dc23
LC record available at http://lccn.loc.gov/2015044004

ISBN: 978-1-138-99830-8 (hbk)
ISBN: 978-1-138-99831-5 (pbk)
ISBN: 978-1-315-65875-9 (ebk)

Typeset in Optima
by Florence Production Ltd, Stoodleigh, Devon

Contents

eResources

The appendices can be downloaded and printed for your own use. You can access these downloads by visiting the book product page on our website: www.routledge.com/books/details/9781138998315. Then click on the tab that says "eResources," and select the files. They will begin downloading to your computer.

Appendix A: Collaborative Learning Team Agenda

Appendix B: Backward Planner Template

Appendix C: SIP Template

Appendix D: SIP Feedback

Appendix E: Feedback Examples from Monitoring SIP

Appendix F: Thought for the Week Examples

Appendix G: Data Analysis Guide

Acknowledgements

Gratitude has been defined as the sense of feeling *helped, saved,* or *seen*. I am grateful for being *helped*:

- Throughout my career numerous individuals have helped me, too many to mention here, but I need to acknowledge my mentor Nancy Mooney. Nancy's intellect, patience, and willingness to share her expertise defined my career and inspired many of the ideas and processes found in this book. Her work lives on even though she can no longer be with us.

I am grateful for being *saved* by the power of working with extremely talented and dedicated leaders:

- Garry Milbourn, Mark Schuldt, and Julie Smith's approach to the work taught me a thing or two and their ongoing friendship continues to brighten my life.
- My co-author Kim Morrison's saves are many. Her work, friendship, and belief in me have made me a better person in all aspects of my life. Such a gift to write this with her.

I am grateful for being *seen*:

- To the publishers at Routledge who saw that we had something important to say even though there are many books on leadership.
- To my parents and siblings who have shaped how I have been seen throughout my life and continue to see the good in me. A special thanks

to my sister Peggy, an accomplished journalist; her support and unwavering belief that I am a fellow writer have provided me with much solace.

- To my sons Jack and Mark, who see me as Mom which in and of itself is enough. Finally, to my husband Tim. From the start he has seen all of me and continues to love, support, and humor me through all of life's journeys.

Ann T. Mausbach

Mirrors are made of glass and they are fragile. It's important that we remember that we are more than one glance; we are reflections of those around us and together we can change the world. There are many excellent principals who reflect excellence and quality; most especially Garry Milbourn and Mark Schuldt are two of the best I've known. I reflect my mother Carolyn, my children, Samantha, Max and Leo. They have taught me to remember what matters most in life: love, loyalty and family. I share this book with my husband Andrzej, who gave me his last name; it would not be possible without his support and partnership. Finally, I hold to mirror in acknowledgement of my partner Dr. Ann T. Mausbach. She is a guiding hand who has provided so many opportunities and is instrumental in my own personal and professional growth.

Kimberly Morrison

Meet the Authors

Ann T. Mausbach currently serves as an Assistant Professor for Educational Leadership at Creighton University. Prior to this position Ann served as an assistant superintendent for curriculum and instruction for fourteen years. Her other central office administrative experience includes serving as a coordinator of staff development, director of curriculum, and director of elementary education. She has twenty years of central office experience.

Ann is co-author of the book *Align the Design* (2008), published by ASCD. She has written for ASCD Express and co-authored a chapter in *Changing Minds, Changing Schools, Changing Systems*, published by Hameray Publishing in 2014. An article she co-authored on improving graduation rates was published in the February 2015 issue of *Educational Leadership*.

Kimberly Morrison is the principal of an urban middle school located in the Midwest. Her administrative experience has included elementary and district administration for over fifteen years. She was named Iowa Middle Level School Administrator of the Year in 2015. She has primarily worked in at-risk environments addressing complicated issues of poverty, homelessness, and special education. She has been the coordinator for new teacher induction, McKinney Vento Homeless Grant and Safe and Drug Free Schools.

1 Introduction

You have to get up and plant the seed and see if it grows, but you can't just wait around, you have to water it and take care of it.
                                                        Bootsy Collins

Gardening requires lots of water—most of it in the form of perspiration.
                                                        Lou Erickson

Did you know that peonies won't grow if you move them or that adding sugar to the soil makes tomatoes sweeter?

If you are a gardener you will realize that these are old wives' tales that aren't true and have been circulating for generations. What does this have to do with leadership, specifically school leadership? Gardens and schools or districts are complex systems and as such require a lot of care. And like gardening myths, myths about leadership continue to circulate, such as the notion that leaders must possess the skills of a superhero, being able to swoop in and solve any problem at any time. Or that leadership is instinctual, you are either born to lead or not. Gardening and leadership are hard enough without falling prey to these falsehoods. The job of the leader, like that of the gardener, is to develop supports and structures that help everyone in the system grow and develop. This requires knowing not only what to do, but when to do it. The complexity of leading a school and a school system filled with adults and students with diverse needs is analogous to tending to the variety of plants that line garden beds. Gardens and school systems prosper when control is balanced by equal measures of commitment and skill (knowing what to do, how to do it, and when to do it). The purpose of this book is to share critical commitments and identify specific practices that operationalize these commitments so they can be skillfully implemented in the context of a school year.

Understanding and making a commitment is far easier than upholding one. Like the well-intentioned gardener who fails to water and weed on a regular basis, school leaders can also get sidetracked from their main job of leading teaching and learning. Commitments get broken when specific practices and processes aren't in place. And even when these practices are in place, without a leader's continual analysis of what is working and what isn't and then adjusting practices, a breakdown will happen. The challenge for school leaders is not in committing to the work, but in making the work happen and continuously thinking about how to improve or refine practices. Figure 1.1 provides a framework to help both principals and central office administrators conceptualize the leadership mindset required to improve a system. The practices that support the commitments are titled "have to dos" and serve to hold up the commitments.

The work of improving a school or system is not a linear process. The gardening analogy is used throughout the book because it helps illustrate the cyclical nature of the work. This book is designed to help show the

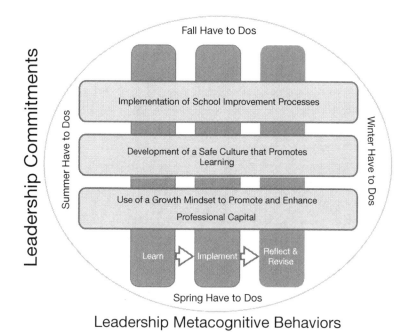

Figure 1.1 Leadership Framework

integrative nature of all three commitments through a series of moves that are connected. Section I outlines the commitments that need to be made, while Section II is designed to explain the moves that need to happen to uphold commitments.

Committing to the Work

One of the compelling findings of Fullan's (2011) research on change is that behaviors change before shifts in beliefs occur. Changing behavior helps to change thinking (Sinek, 2015). Commitment happens when new experiences are provided that allow individuals to practice and build on the learning. It is in the "doing" that sincere changes in beliefs occur. It's a bit like the Nike ads, "Just do it." Do the work, and the belief and dedication to the change will follow. Leaders wanting to have an impact on an entire school or system need to understand that this finding is a call to action not only for how to approach work with staff, but how to approach their daily work. Commit to the work by engaging in behaviors that will transform beliefs and ultimately the system. Committing to the work requires a high degree of persistence. A dedicated gardener sticks with it even when the plants don't sprout up right away, or the rabbits eat their lettuce. Leadership is also a practice that requires a high degree of commitment in order to get results. Consistency is more important than intensity (Sinek, 2015).

But what should school leaders be committing to? Commitments stem from knowing what is valued. Value defines purpose. The purpose of a garden is growth so gardeners value the land and the weather. The purpose of schooling is student learning, so school leaders need to value the people and processes that make this happen. School leaders need to commit to:

- Implementation of school improvement processes at high levels.
- Development of a school culture that promotes learning.
- Use of a growth mindset to develop and enhance professional capital.

These commitments stem from the three components that make up the professional capital equation; human, social, and decisional capital (Hargreaves & Fullan, 2012). Professional capital is a framework for leading learning that involves equal measure and interaction of the three types of capital in order to develop the entire organization. Human capital, which has for too long been the focus in schools and school systems, pertains to individual talent. Are there skilled teachers and principals in the system? Social capital refers to the quality and quantity of social interactions in schools. How often and how well do teachers and principals collaborate?

Decisional capital refers to the ability to make good decisions and judgments based on experience and learning. How are decisions made when the answers aren't clear-cut? Improving, using, and connecting all three capitals creates a balanced system and promotes school reform. In a balanced system groups work together in such a way that it improves the performance of the individual. The group changes both the group and the individual for the better. Decisions are made based on professional judgment that has been honed through working together through a variety of situations. Gardening is a symbiotic process that relies on the interaction of various conditions such as plants, soil, and weather. Each condition interplays with the others in the same sense that professional capital does. All three capitals interact with each other to develop healthy professional capital.

Commitment is defined as the state or quality of being that is dedicated to a cause, activity, etc. The cause for leaders in schools must be developing professional capital. Committing to implementing school improvement processes dedicates the leader's actions to improving decisional capital, development of a school culture that promotes learning improves social capital, and using a growth mindset to develop and enhance professional capital helps increase human capital.

Section I of this book outlines the three commitments that leaders must make to improve schools. The relationship between each commitment and one aspect of professional capital is outlined. Critical concepts that underpin each commitment are discussed. Specific actions that a leader should and shouldn't do when thinking through these concepts are included and titled "do this," "not that." Each chapter ends with a story from both the building and district level to help illustrate the commitment in action. Look for the school house icon which indicates the "Commitment to Action".

Doing the Work

A master gardener is both committed and skilled. The gardener's skill is in knowing what must be done when and using the right tools to make the work happen. Gardeners understand that each season of the year is a distinct period of time marked by specific weather conditions, temperatures, and length of day. These variables define the growing season. Although each season represents a unique period that requires specific behaviors and actions, the cycles are recursive and interdependent. For example, the harvest in the fall is a result of the planting in the spring and the weather conditions in the summer. Skilled gardeners also understand the interconnectedness between soil, seeds, and maintenance. The garden can be well designed with straight rows that have seeds planted at exact distances but there will be little harvest if it isn't watered, weeded, and fertilized.

And so it goes for school leaders. Leaders must understand the seasons of the school year and engage in specific behaviors at critical points in the year, using the right tools at the right time. For schools, summer marks the season for reflection and planning. During these months leaders are busy making sure they have the right infrastructure in place, in terms of both schedules and human resources, to do the work. The fall is when the planting begins. Leaders prepare the field by making sure they have school improve-ment and professional development plans that align with a strong mission and vision. Finally, during the winter/spring, schools focus on making sure that they are getting the right results with an ongoing focus on implementation.

Section II of this book outlines the specific "have to dos" principals and central office administrators need to complete during each season of the year in order to ensure that the three commitments are operationalized. Principal and central office moves for the "have to dos" have been identified in order to help leaders prioritize the work. Just because the "have to dos" have been associated with a certain season doesn't preclude them being used throughout the year. The "have to dos" identified have been paired with a particular season because they make up the preponderance of the work that should occur at that time of the year. Reflective questions are included at the end of each "have to do" to help the leader discern next steps. These questions have been differentiated so that leaders just beginning to use these practices and those that have had some experience can focus on the right things. At the end of each chapter there is a "Planting Seeds" story. This story is one that the authors have used in the past to motivate staff in weekly communications and is included to help reiterate the main points of the chapter. Table 1.1 outlines the "have to dos" and principal and central office moves for each season. Look for the runner icon which indicates the "Principal and Central Office Moves".

Table 1.1 Overview of "Have to Dos" and Leader Moves

Have to Dos	Principal Moves	Central Office Moves
	FALL	
Engage staff in developing/revising a plan for improvement	Move 1: Create an organizational structure that enables all staff buy in Move 2: Utilize data to develop/revise plan Move 3: Revise/revisit the mission	Move 1: Develop/use common template Move 2: Provide training to principals Move 3: Give feedback on individual building plans
Develop look fors	Move 4: Collaboratively define look fors Move 5: Provide feedback using look fors	Move 4: Provide feedback on feedback and look fors
Differentiate supervision for staff	Move 6: Align individual growth plans to SIP Move 7: Monitor feedback efforts	Move 5: Provide coaching visits to principals
	WINTER	
Monitor the plan	Move 1: Schedule and conduct general and focused walkthroughs Move 2: Use displays of student work to reinforce learning	Move 1: Conduct supervisory walkthroughs using school's look fors Move 2: Use weekly communication to principals to reinforce district initiatives
Develop teachers by responding to individual needs	Move 3: Use PLCs to support students and teachers	Move 3: Provide infrastructure of support by defining quality Move 4: Use resources strategically
Embed the mission in the work	Move 4: Use the mission as a lens for revising and adopting new initiatives	Move 5: Reinforce the use of mission with principals through reflective practice

Have to Dos	Principal Moves	Central Office Moves
	SPRING	
Stay the course while planning ahead	Move: Monitor instruction Move: Benchmark progress on school improvement efforts (gathering data)	Move: Identify and communicate instructional focus for upcoming year
Support professional learning	Move: Evaluate staff using supervision practices Move: Develop/revisit infrastructure for professional learning	Move: Develop a year-long professional learning plan for principals Move: Plan summer learning opportunities for teachers
Recognize improvement	Move: Celebrate accomplishments through reflection Move: Plan transitions for students	Move: Identify district growth through a summative analysis
	SUMMER	
Conduct a summative analysis of the data	Move: Develop a data portfolio and participate in a data consult	Move: Conduct data consults
Reflect and respond	Move: Read and think	Move: Review and revise district curriculum
Tend to the environment	Move: Create an invitational setting	Move: Provides resources necessary for safe and inviting settings

Book Overview

Section I: Sowing the Field: Commitments

Chapter 2: Implementation of School Improvement Processes at High Levels

This chapter describes the patient labor and attention that must be given to the five core processes of school improvement. An overview of the blue-print processes for school improvement is shared (Mooney & Mausbach, 2008). An emphasis is placed on the importance of focus, alignment, and the use of proper tools to implement processes. A discussion on how the use of these processes helps to promote professional capital is included. An example of how this commitment was put into action in an elementary school in order to improve literacy is provided. The use of feedback as an exemplar of the commitment in action is shared from the district perspective.

Chapter 3: Development of a Safe Culture that Promotes Learning

Attention and focus must be placed on both the academics of a school and the culture. Both features are critically important to school success. Chapter 3 reinforces the priority that must be placed on building a healthy culture. An explanation of how a focus on a healthy culture promotes social capital is shared. The importance of relationships, developing a safe and engaging environment and creating an invitational setting are critical concepts that are explored. A process called clipboard discipline is shared as an example of the commitment in action at the school level. Using student displays of work and writing to shift a culture at the district level is the example on how to uphold this commitment.

Chapter 4: Use of a Growth Mindset to Develop and Enhance Professional Capital

The focus for Chapter 4 is on growth. A description of a growth mindset and the relationship with developing human capital is included. Leaders use a growth mindset when they create a culture of collaborative inquiry, focus on content and process learning, and use feedback for improvement. The process for how a building's collaborative processes evolved will be shared to illustrate this commitment in action. Structuring opportunities for principal growth will be shared as a district practice.

Section II: Seasons: Working the Field to Yield Higher Results

Chapter 5: Fall: Starting the Year with Clarity and Focus

Fall is a busy time of year in the school business. In order to get the school year off to a good start and to ensure that the system is headed in the right direction, leaders need to make sure that they engage staff in school improvement planning, develop shared meaning with staff on the plan, and align supervision of staff with school improvement processes. Chapter 5 shares the principal and central office moves associated with accomplishing these "have to dos."

Chapter 6: Winter: Making the Work Happen through Implementation and Monitoring

During the winter, school leaders uphold commitments by staying focused on and expanding the work that was started in the fall. Through the winter "have to dos" leaders will learn how to use walkthroughs to monitor school improvement work, how to work with staff to meet individual needs, and how to keep the mission alive and relevant. Principal and central office moves are shared that help define how to make sure the work gets done.

Chapter 7: Spring: Staying the Course While Looking Forward

Spring is a time when students and staff can get restless. The great weather and approaching end of the school year can become distractions. During the spring, leaders need to start planning for the upcoming year, while staying the course with school improvement efforts. Keeping professional learning front and center during this time is critical. During the spring it is also important to recognize and honor improvement and achievements throughout the year. Specific moves for principals and central office leaders that help ensure these "have to dos" are in place will be shared.

Chapter 8: Summer: Reflecting, Refining, and Planning

The summer months provide school leaders with the necessary time to take pause and do some deep thinking around the actions in the previous seasons. Leaders need to take a hard look at summative data and reflect on and respond to what they have learned. Summer is also a time to tend to the physical environment so that an invitational setting is created for students and staff. Specific moves for principals and central office staff are outlined that help leaders accomplish these tasks.

Emily Hughes (2015) tells a story in her children's book titled *The Little Gardener* of a boy who is frustrated and overwhelmed with the enormous task of caring for his garden. He loves his garden, it means the world to him, but his small size and how much work needs to be done to make it thrive discourage him. However, one plant blooms and this plant gives hope to others who see it and who in the end join him in helping create a beautiful and wondrous garden. It is easy to get overwhelmed by the enormous task of caring for and nurturing a whole school or school system of students. Leaders can feel small and inconsequential in their attempts to make improvements. But, like the little gardener, leaders must not lose hope. Hope is not a plan, but it can help ordinary people do extraordinary things. This book is designed to give leaders hope by providing them tools to plant seeds of excellence, inspiring and engaging those around them. Being a school leader is hard work, but also rewarding. The commitments and "have to dos" outlined in this book help the leader realize this reward and see that the fruits of their labor make a real difference in the lives of children.

References

Fullan, M. (2011). *The six secrets of change: What the best leaders do to help their organizations survive and thrive.* San Francisco, CA: Jossey-Bass.

Hargreaves, A. & Fullan, M. (2012). *Professional capital: Transforming teaching in every school.* New York: Teachers College Press & Toronto: Ontario Principals Council.

Hughes, E. (2015). *The little gardener.* London: Flying Eye Books.

Mooney, N. & Mausbach, A. (2008). *Align the design: A blueprint for school improvement.* Alexandria, VA: Association for Supervision of Curriculum and Development.

Sinek, S. (2015). *Lecture: Leaders eat last: Why some teams come together and others don't* [video]. www.sai-iowa.org/leaders-eat-last-book-study.cfm

Sowing the Field

Commitments

Implementation of School Improvement Processes at High Levels

A garden requires patient labor and attention. Plants do not grow merely to satisfy ambitions or to fulfill good intentions. They thrive because someone expended effort on them.

Liberty Hyde Bailey

Understanding the patient labor and attention needed to have a thriving garden helps describe the commitment required by leaders to school improvement processes. A bountiful garden doesn't just happen. Gardening is a deliberate process. The gardener starts with a clear vision for what they want to sow. Once this is identified, a suitable plot is found, taking into account the soil and location. Before rushing in and planting, the skilled gardener takes time to design the garden, giving careful consideration to where different vegetables or fruits will be planted, how far apart the rows need to be, and the depth the variety of seeds need to be planted. After all of this is done, the gardener plants the seeds and maintains the garden by tending to it on a frequent basis. Maintenance requires skill on the gardener's part so that only weeds get pulled and fertilizer is applied appropriately. The degree to which a gardener attends to the soil, design, planting and ongoing upkeep determines the abundance of the harvest. The interdependency between the soil, seeds, upkeep, and weather conditions determines the success of the garden.

Improving a school is also a deliberate process that requires planning and attention. Mooney and Mausbach (2008) identified five core processes, that they titled blueprint processes for school improvement, that mirror the actions of successful gardeners. These processes are as follows:

1. Establishing a mission, vision, and values that guide the general direction of the school and its future actions.

2. Using data analysis, which includes both collecting and interpreting data, for decision-making.

3. Using a school improvement plan to guide goals, strategies, action steps, and decisions in order to create a working plan for the school.

4. Implementing professional development that serves as the engine for the school improvement plan.

5. Differentiating supervision of teaching and learning to monitor how processes are working in classrooms.

Like the master gardener, the effective school leader understands that it is the interconnectedness of these processes that determines the success of the school. If one of the core processes is missing (e.g., differentiated supervision of the plan), then the results will not be as desired. Figure 2.1 provides an overview of the processes and their relationship.

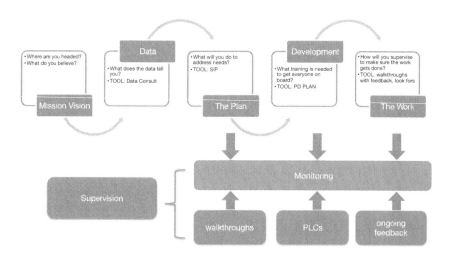

Figure 2.1 Blueprint Processes for School Improvement

Commitment as Development of Professional Capital—Decisional Capital

Decisional capital is one of the three functions of professional capital, as noted in Chapter 1. Professional capital, according to Hargreaves and Fullan (2012), is the key to large-scale change and requires equal measures of decisional, human, and social capital. Decisional capital is the ability to make good decisions so that human and social capital are used most effectively. This requires a leader to use knowledge, intellect, and experience to make decisions. Decisional capital increases as the process for making decisions expands from the individual to the group. Professional judgment becomes more powerful when the decision-making skills of individuals and groups work in tandem (Fullan, 2014). Like its counterparts human and social capital, improving or increasing decisional capital must be a deliberate process. Leaders who commit to implementing school improvement processes at high levels are using and refining decisional capital. Decisional capital helps to ensure the quality and monitoring of school improvement processes.

This commitment requires leaders to use school improvement processes as the lens for decision-making. Using the mission to help determine what data to collect, identifying professional development practices based on the strategies in the school improvement plan, and using look fors to determine what to observe in classrooms are just a few examples of how these processes focus decision-making. Each process requires the leader to collaborate with staff to make decisions about the direction of the school, enhancing the decision-making skills of the group. Decisions made throughout the cycle of school improvement have a direct impact on how resources will be used and how staff work together. Committing to implementing school improvement processes at high levels is not just a nice concept that a leader should consider; it is imperative and essential to moving a school forward, as it influences decisional capital, which in turn has a positive effect on both the human and social capital of the organization.

Indicators of Critical Concepts and Commitment in Practice

Making a commitment is akin to making a promise. Many times, vows accompany a commitment, such as in a wedding ceremony. Vows are expressed to demonstrate how the promise will be kept. Leaders need to vow to observe certain practices and behaviors in order to uphold the commitment to implementing school improvement processes at high levels. Conversely, there are behaviors and practices that prohibit upholding this promise. Leaders need to embrace three critical concepts and adopt certain practices that will help the commitment be manifested in their daily work. The critical concepts include the following:

- *Alignment* of all of the processes for school improvement is necessary for sustained improvement.
- A fundamental purpose of the school improvement plan is to provide *focus*.
- There are specific *tools* that help with alignment and focus.

Alignment

Alignment of school improvement processes is when all of the processes (mission/vision, data, the plan, professional development and supervision) work in concert. Translating the vision of the organization into a reality by setting a direction that results in whole school consistency and high expectations is one of the core functions of system leadership (Leithwood, Day, Sammons, Harris, & Hopkins, 2006). Aligning the mission and vision of the school into a data-driven focused school improvement and professional development plan that is continually monitored and supervised is how leaders get this done. Alignment happens when the leader has the mindset that everything in the organization is instrumental to the achievement of collective goals. Rather than looking outside of the organization for improvement levers, leaders look within and work to align the processes and resources in a systematic and focused way (Elmore, 2008).

Many times, schools and districts believe they have alignment because they have several of these processes in place. For example, a mission statement may exist; schools have improvement plans and engage in data analysis. However, these processes are done in isolation of each other, treated as separate activities rather than actions that must interosculate in order to get maximum results. In a misaligned system, plans don't refer back to the mission and vision and the professional development provided has limited, if any, connection to the plan. Misalignment can also look like a school operating with several "school improvement" plans. For example, if a school is a Title I school there may be a plan that addresses those needs, a plan required by their state if they aren't hitting achievement targets, a plan to address the needs of special populations, etc. In a misaligned system data analysis may occur, but rarely does it result in goal setting or action steps in the school improvement plan. Alignment requires deliberate attention to the core processes and an unwavering commitment to making sure they are connected.

Do This

Think in terms of how decisions and actions connect to the mission and overall goals of the school.

One of the questions a leader should continually pose to themselves is, "Does this decision or action connect or fragment the work?" Even though this work is extremely collaborative it falls upon the leader's shoulders to assure that all the dots are connected in the school improvement puzzle. Without this, a leader and their team can work diligently all year on a number of important issues only to end up at the end of the year wondering why the vision for the school hasn't become a reality. Much like the distorted picture that is the result of a dot to dot puzzle that didn't correctly connect the numbers, the same thing can happen for a school without tight alignment. The leader needs to be vigilant and deliberate, working through and bridging the processes to each other through decisions and actions every day. Section II will provide more specifics on these actions.

Not That

Treat school improvement as isolated activities or an event.

"Event-like" school improvement looks like only addressing the mission at the beginning of the year or only looking at data at the end of the year. When school improvement processes are isolated, supervision of teachers is an activity that happens three times a year (or less) and is prescribed by a form rather than improvement strategies. Plans are developed to satisfy higher ups (either at the district or state level) and are an administrative exercise rather than a collaborative undertaking. The savvy conductor knows that it takes all of the instruments in the orchestra working together to make beautiful music. The savvy school leader understands this as well, and though different processes may need more fine tuning at different times of the year, it is only when they consociate that improvements in student achievement can be realized.

Focus

Intense focus requires leaders to have a laser-like commitment to a clearly defined path for school improvement. Focus requires a steadfast commitment to a limited number of improvement strategies and a steady resolve to avoid succumbing to the razzle and dazzle of new initiatives. Large-scale improvement doesn't happen without a tight instructional focus sustained over time (Elmore, 2008). Focus happens when what is of essential importance in the context of the organization is identified and efforts are concentrated on these essentials. Schools that set goals and use them to coordinate the work of the adults in the school around teaching and learning see their focused efforts result in higher student achievement (Robinson, 2014). A lack of focus has the same catastrophic results as the garden that isn't weeded. Competing initiatives vie for teachers' time and attention and result in frantic activity that leads nowhere. Doing too many things at once without an aligned focus results in repeated failure, overwhelming teachers and administrators who become increasingly confused and frustrated (Kotter, 2008). The school improvement plan must help provide clarity and coherence by identifying a limited number of goals, strategies, and action steps based on the needs of the school. The litmus test for an effective school improvement plan lies in the number of goals and strategies included. A litany of goals indicates lack of focus. Leaders need to use the processes for developing the plan, aligning the mission vision and data, to help them develop a concise and focused improvement plan.

Do This

Say no.

One of the simplest ways that a school or system can get and stay focused is by saying no. One of the reasons why being a school administrator is such hard work is because it can feel like an endless game of whack-a-mole. Whack-a-mole is the carnival game that has little moles popping up while the player tries to whack them back into their holes only to have them continue to surface. Leading a school or system can feel this same way as a leader is in perpetual reaction mode, which is what happens when there isn't focus. Schools are complex organizations, which is one of the reasons why focus can be so difficult. Lucky for us we have great examples of other complex organizations that have been widely successful due to their ability to focus. One of the core philosophies that Steve Jobs identified when creating Apple was to focus on the important and eliminate the unimportant. Apple is successful because the company focuses on a handful of products and obsesses over getting those right. Apple's approach to business exemplifies Kluger's (2009) concept of simplexity. Simplexity is the ability to focus on a small number of ambitious goals and factors (simple part) and make them gel (complex part). Achieving simplexity requires a leader to be clear about what they will and won't do. This requires a leader to say no when activities or initiatives will take them away from their core focus.

Not That

Let compliance be the driver for reform.

Far too many schools and districts allow mandates from outside the organization to set the direction. To be clear, complying with federal and state requirements is important and the authors are not advocating that these shouldn't be met. What we are advocating is that these should not be the drivers for reform or used to determine focus. Leaders need to be compliant to the requirements, but that doesn't mean they need to use planning forms or follow lockstep professional development presentations handed down from the state. Effective leaders make sense of the new information by determining how and when to integrate it into their current system; they ask themselves how the requirements align with their current focus and what if any minor changes need to be made to their processes. Rather than treating these as the centerpiece on a beautifully set table they view them as a utensil that supports the overall aesthetic.

Tools

Having and using the proper tools is not a luxury, but a necessity. A gardener would never attempt to till soil without the proper tools. Without a hoe or a power tiller it is easy to see how difficult planting would be and why a gardener might get frustrated and give up. Using the power tools for school improvement can reduce the frustration that many administrators face. The process of improvement requires changes in the structure, processes, and norms for how the work is organized (Kegan & Lahey, 2002). The power tools of school improvement help create this change and when used properly increase the knowledge and skill of the people in the organization. Power tools identified by Mooney and Mausbach (2008) include a data consult and data portfolio, a focused school improvement and professional development plan, look fors, walkthroughs with feedback, and differentiated supervision practices (see Figure 2.1). These tools help the leader operationalize school improvement processes. When used on a regular basis, the power tools, which will be described in length in Section II of the book, help the organization move through the improvement continuum. Administrators who use these processes over time frequently comment on how rudimentary their first school improvement plan or set of look fors was compared to more recent efforts. Refinement happens through repeated use, demonstrating the developmental nature of school improvement.

Do This

Use the tools frequently.

School improvement is a developmental process that means that high performance and quality aren't an event; rather they are a point along a continuum. Schools may be at varying points along this developmental continuum and practices of improvement may vary by stages; however, the practice of improvement in general requires mastery of practices across stages (Elmore, 2008). Thus, how the tools are used may look different along different points on the improvement continuum, but the tools are essential at every stage. At the beginning stages the tools may feel cumbersome and more prescriptive in nature. As the school moves along the continuum and practices are refined, tools will feel more integrated and will be used seamlessly throughout the school. The key is to continue to use the tools even when they feel clunky. Learning is the work (Fullan, 2008). As leaders and their teams use the tools to achieve the goals of the system, learning will occur. This learning is embedded in the context of the work and will result in refinements to how the tools are being used.

Not That

Ignore the developmental nature of school improvement.

Moving a school along the continuum of improvement requires the leader to understand the varying stages that occur. Leaders need to adjust their practices as the organization moves along the continuum. Thus, a leader needs to be cognizant of how to monitor and adjust the use of school improvement tools so they are the most efficient in the context of the school at that particular stage. This means that learning must be continuous. The tools can stand alone, but a savvy leader who has used them over time understands that when they are interwoven into practice, improvement accelerates. Leaders' knowledge and skill expand as the school improves. Leaders know that they must use the tools to sustain focus as they work with staff to tackle more progressively complex problems of practice.

Putting this commitment into action takes concentrated and deliberate effort. An example of how an elementary school implemented school improvement process at high levels in order to improve literacy is provided in the next section. Focusing a district on committing to implementation of school improvement processes from a district perspective follows the building example.

Building Level Commitment in Action: One Building, One Plan

The Issue

The elementary school of 420 students, 85 percent receiving free and reduced lunch, had stagnant achievement. For approximately five years only 48 percent of the students were proficient in reading comprehension on state exams and national percentile scores hovered around the 30th percentile. The building had a Title I plan, a special education plan, and a School In Need of Assistance (SINA) plan as designated by the state due to low performance. Each plan had a few goals and several action steps. The goals were based on content area improvement but weren't connected and weren't linked to data. A litany of activities that were all-encompassing and difficult to implement and monitor were identified and submitted to central office, never to be reviewed again. Another plan for professional development was developed separately from the school improvement plans and was based entirely on a state and district initiative. The principal knew through classroom observations that reading instruction varied from classroom to classroom and that even though teachers had some training on guided reading groups they lacked an understanding of other essential components in a strong literacy program. Reading was extremely difficult for students, as evidenced by their unwillingness to read for pleasure and their inability to use strategies to monitor comprehension. In order to address this critical need, the leader knew that a laser-like focus on effective reading instruction was necessary.

The Response

A focused school improvement plan with a clear goal, strategies, and action steps addressing literacy was necessary. The school improvement plan developed around a strategy of implementing mini lessons in a reading workshop. This strategy was selected for two reasons. First, students were disengaged in the reading process and lacked strategies for success. Second, although the district had adopted the partnership for comprehensive literacy model from the University of Arkansas, Little Rock (Dorn & Soffos, 2005) the previous year, it was clear through the principal's walkthroughs and professional learning community (PLC) meetings that teachers were struggling with implementing rigorous mini lessons. In addition to this plan a professional development plan was developed that outlined the learning needed to implement the strategy. Following are the goal, strategy, action steps, and professional development for the plan.

To monitor the plan, the principal used the collaboratively developed look fors listed below to provide teachers with feedback. Clearly articulating when the strategy was observed in classroom practice worked to reinforce the importance of the professional development plan. The principal observed in every classroom every week and provided feedback via a weekly blog validating examples of look fors observed in classrooms.

Sample look fors:

- Teacher uses intentional/precise language; provides a singular, clear curricular objective that includes purpose and application.
- Teacher uses a mentor text to teach concept.
- Students have an opportunity to apply learning (i.e., turn and talk) before being asked to do it independently.

Goal

Improve reading comprehension as evidenced by:

- 87 percent reading comprehension proficiency on ITBS in February '12
- Growth in NPR by 5 percentile points on ITBS in February '12

Strategy

Implement reader's workshop with a focus on quality mini lesson.

Action Steps

1. Study/review the moves of a focus/mini lesson.

2. Develop a rubric/look fors to monitor mini lesson implementation and provide feedback.

3. Collaboratively plan mini lessons in PLCs based on grade level curriculum.

4. Use the literacy planning guide within all workshops using literacy resources to guide planning of mini lessons.

5. Examine student work in reading and writing to determine impact of mini lesson.

6. Conduct an implementation study of mini/focus lesson.

Professional Development

1. Whole group: Provide rationale, implementation data for mini lesson.

2. Small group: Study a model of mini lesson, i.e. Teaching for Deep Comprehension.

3. Whole group: Develop a list of moves and criteria for mini lesson.

4. Small group planning: Study student work, observe video of mini lessons.

5. Individual: Work with principal for refinement of implementation.

- Mini lesson ends by teacher restating how this can be used when reading.
- Lesson is 10–15 minutes in length.
- Co-constructed anchor charts posted and referenced during the lesson.

Results

After three years of implementing the literacy goal, 81 percent of students were proficient in reading comprehension on the state exam. Over the three years 79 percent of low SES and 62 percent of special education students met proficiency targets. National percentile rank moved from the low 40s to the mid 60s. The once failing school was now off "the list" and, better yet, students not only knew how to read, but wanted to read.

District Level Commitment in Action: School Improvement as Feedback

Issue

In the district of approximately 10,000 students, demographics were shifting. Mobility rates and the percentage of students living in poverty were steadily increasing every year, specifically in one half of the district. Achievement across the district on state assessments was stagnant, but was showing more decline in the higher poverty schools. In an effort to respond to this situation the schools with higher percentages of free and reduced lunch students developed improvement plans due to their Title I status. The plans were developed in isolation and principals had limited direction as to how to develop an effective plan. These plans were submitted to central office as part of Title I compliance and filed away. Monitoring of the plans occurred at the end of the year.

Response

The newly hired Assistant Superintendent for Curriculum and Instruction knew a systemic approach was needed in order to address achievement issues. Understanding the influence principals have on student achieve-ment, efforts were concentrated on helping them develop a solid under-standing of school improvement processes and the tools that support the work. A multiyear plan for professional development was phased in. During year one principals learned how to develop a school improvement and professional development plan. Principals were trained on how to use a common template, and written feedback was provided once plans were submitted. Principals also learned the process of walkthroughs and how to develop look fors. Twice a year the Assistant Superintendent visited the schools and conducted supervisory walkthroughs looking for evidence of implementation of the school improvement plan based on the school's look fors. During principals' monthly professional development sessions they worked in small groups sharing their overall plans and plan progress throughout the year.

The next phase for learning for the principals was around how to use data to align school improvement efforts. Principals participated in summer training and were taught how to develop a data portfolio. Principals developed a data portfolio and participated in data consults. They received written feedback after the consults designed to help ensure that school improvement strategies addressed needs uncovered during the data consult. Supervisory walkthroughs continued to look for evidence of implementation of the school improvement plan, and principals collaborated monthly on plan progress and roadblocks. The final phase of training focused on align-ing the mission and using differentiated supervision practices, specifically learning teams.

Results

While achievement results began to improve, three important shifts took place in terms of leadership. First, principals were more focused in their efforts to improve the school. They began to understand the continuous nature of school improvement and the process moved from being an isolated activity completed to meet compliance requirements to a core function of the school. Second, principals became more collaborative with each other. The common language and processes coupled with collaborative time during monthly professional development made it easier for principals to share successes, challenges, and "ahas." Finally, the perception of the central office administrator changed. Principals began to see this person as a support and resource rather than someone who issued directives.

References

Dorn, L. J., & Soffos, C. (2005). *Teaching for deep comprehension: A workshop approach*. Portland, ME: Stenhouse Publishers.

Elmore, R. F. (2008). Leadership as the practice of improvement. In Pont, B., Nusche, D., & Hopkins, D. (Eds.), *Improving school leadership, volume 2: Case studies on system leadership* (pages 21–25), 2nd ed. Paris: Organisation for Economic Co-operation and Development.

Fullan, M. (2008). *The six secrets of change: What the best leaders do to help their organizations survive and thrive*. San Francisco, CA: Jossey-Bass.

Fullan, M. (2014). *The principal: Three keys to maximizing impact*. San Francisco, CA: Jossey-Bass.

Hargreaves, A., & Fullan, M. (2012). *Professional capital: Transforming teaching in every school*. New York: Teachers College Press.

Kegan, R., & Lahey, L. (2002). *How the way we talk can change the way we work: Seven languages for transformation*. San Francisco, CA: Jossey-Bass.

Kluger, J. (2009). *Simplexity: Why simple things become complex (and how complex things can become simple)*. New York: Hyperion Books.

Kotter, J. (2008). *A sense of urgency*. Boston, MA: Harvard Business Press.

Leithwood, K., Day, C., Sammons, P., Harris, A., & Hopkins, D. (2006). *Seven strong claims about successful school leadership*. National College for School Leadership/Department of Education and Skills, Nottingham.

Mooney, N., & Mausbach, A. (2008). *Align the design: A blueprint for school improvement*. Alexandria, VA: Association for Supervision of Curriculum and Development.

Robinson, V. M. J. (2014). *Student-centered leadership*. Hoboken, NJ: Jossey-Bass.

3

Development of a Safe Culture that Promotes Learning

If you look the right way, you can see that the whole world is a garden.
Frances Hodgson Burnett, *The Secret Garden*

Imagine walking into a beautiful garden. You are immediately confronted with a symphony of smells, sounds, and visual experiences. You notice everything and this first impression influences your senses and how you feel. There are many elements that you can focus on: the aromatic blooms, the splashes of color, the loamy scent of the earth. You hear the buzz of insects and the song of birds. You may instantly feel a sense of peace, happiness, or have triggered a memory from your childhood. Everything that you are experiencing is a result of the planting, season, tools, fertilizer, animal life, and work of the gardener.

School culture can be experienced in a similar way. It is what we breathe, smell, and hear as we walk into the environment. A positive culture will manifest feelings of welcome, warmth, and an assumed belief of positive achievement. A toxic culture may assault the visitor with a cold institutional tone, discourteous staff, and chaotic movements. Culture may seem elusive but it is essential; it is what determines whether we want to linger or flee. School culture is not fixed or immovable. It is continually being shaped and influenced through the interaction of all stakeholders in the environment.

Leaders cannot treat "culture" as an action. It is an outcome of intentional actions taken within a system. The authors found that planning actions around climate and relationships resulted in dramatic changes in the culture. Walking into a building with a healthy culture is analogous to discussing climate with regard to weather. One knows what types of weather to expect within a given season in a particular part of the country. Likewise, there is a sense of what to expect when a visitor walks into a school, i.e., "I will feel welcome here," "I want to learn here because people care and I feel safe." This result isn't something that occurs because something is written on the wall or the principal has "told" staff how to behave. It is created through the consistent behaviors of every staff member over time, which create these conditions. Chenoweth and Theokas state,

> Culture has to do with how the people in the school react to the climate and the daily weather conditions in the building. Do they band together to keep warm in a cold snap or hoard their firewood so that only some survive?
>
> (2011, p. 151)

Culture is a combination of climate and ethos (the emotional connection). Climate is promoted through communicating a clear mission/vision, fostering collaboration, creating an orderly environment, empowering teachers in decision-making, and setting clear expectations for students and teachers. These actions result in a feeling in the school that helps staff connect to the work, sustaining school improvement efforts. Improvement efforts will not be effective, maintained, or enhanced unless school culture and academics are both addressed and aligned (Fisher & Frey, 2012).

 # Commitment as Development of Professional Capital: Social Capital

Social capital is the art of collaborating with others in order to have a positive effect on learning. It is one of three facets of professional capital, as outlined in Chapter 1. To be a game changer in the area of learning a leader must focus on the quality and quantity of interactions that take place in a school or system. Social capital is so powerful because it accesses the individual expertise which helps the group perform at higher levels, increasing human capital. One person's labor in a garden will make a difference, but when a community collaborates on a garden, the yield is much higher. A school or system with high social capital has a high level of trust, common expectations, and a deep sense of responsibility to work together towards a common goal (Fullan, 2014).

This commitment requires leaders to intentionally develop and nurture relationships. Without attention to the types and quality of interactions, a healthy learning culture can't be built. A healthy culture requires cohesion rather than individualistic agendas. Social capital is the mechanism that breaks down silos in a system. Leaders who commit to making sure that the culture in a system is healthy understand and spend considerable time working alongside people, developing a risk-free and welcoming environment.

Indicators of Critical Concepts and Commitment in Practice

Culture is an abstract notion but committing to three fundamental concepts makes it feel more tangible. Leaders need to pledge to certain practices in order to uphold the commitment to influence culture. Pledging to this commitment results in dramatic changes that create impenetrable bonds of loyalty and resilience in staff and students. The following concepts, based on research, help leaders commit to building a healthy culture.

- Culture is built on authentic **relationships** with students and staff.
- A **safe and engaging environment** is fundamental to culture.
- The **invitational environment** contributes to the overall culture of a school.

Relationships

School leaders need to commit to the symbiotic relationship between improving instruction and the culture and climate of the school. Effective leadership is about simultaneously addressing relationships and instruction. Relationships are strengthened through working together to address teaching and learning issues (Robinson, 2011). Positive relationships are the cornerstone of a healthy culture. Staff and students who are emotionally engaged in the work of the school or system are more likely to find success. This type of engagement requires a personal commitment and a shared sense of purpose. Positive relationships are developed when people work together to achieve goals. This can't happen in isolation. In schools with a positive culture there is a shared "ethos of caring and concern" along with a commitment to foster learning (Peterson & Deal, 2009).

Strong relationships provide the motivation for staff to do the hard work of improving a school or system. Teachers are more willing to work for principals who treat them with respect. Relationship is the fuel for motivation. We've all experienced times in our lives when our energy is low and we are ready to give up. What keeps you going? The answer is it depends. If the situation is one where you are working with someone with whom you have a strong personal relationship, you will keep going; however, if there isn't a strong personal relationship, you may throw in the towel. Students will behave and be engaged for teachers who care. Teachers will persevere through a task for principals who take a personal interest. Administrators will endure for supervisors who support and guide them.

Do This

Take care of others.

Sinek (2009) reminds us that leadership isn't about being in charge; it's about taking care of your charge. Taking care of others means understanding the needs of others on both a personal and professional level. Like a parent who puts their children first, so should the leader. And just like in parenting, the level of care will change as the relationships develop. While the level of care may change, it never goes away. Principals develop a deep understanding of a teacher's professional practice and personal interest. In practice this means that a leader understands that when a teacher has had a major life event such as a break-up with a boyfriend or the death of a parent, they need more support. This doesn't mean expectations change, but what it does mean is that in order for the individual to be successful they will need more touches, more feedback, more attention. Leaders realize that when they care and put others' needs first, positive relationships bloom, promoting growth and transformational learning experiences.

Not That

Attend to the task not the person.

An aloof stance conveys a lack of interest in the individual. Perception is reality and even if the harried leader doesn't mean to come off as a snob, that is what occurs when task completion supersedes relationships. A negative impression is difficult to overcome, but can be if there is a connection with the individual. A co-worker will more readily forgive an error when a strong relationship exists. The astute leader is mindful of their body language and voice tone and recognizes how those communicate a state of mind. When eyes wander to a smartphone during a conversation, this speaks volumes about how much more the text is valued than the individual. Leaders must be cognizant of all of their actions large and small as they communicate what is valued.

Safe and Engaging Environment

Academic achievement is impossible without order. Policies, programs, rules, and procedures are mandated and a basic element of a school or system's organizational climate. However, that doesn't mean that these processes are static; they need to be massaged and used as instruments for change. There is a comfort in structure and this is derived from consistency. Consistency requires using organizational tools such as norms, process, and monitoring techniques that are familiar and transparent. The physical safety of students is achieved when clear procedures are outlined, understood, and used. Robinson (2011) contends that in the absence of order it is highly unlikely that achievement will improve. However, if leaders intentionally act to improve safety/order along with instructional goals, improvement is assured.

Engaging classroom environments are a result of high quality teaching and learning. Students feel emotionally safe in these environments because they are consistently doing activities that challenge and interest them. Even when the challenge is high for students they stay engaged. When active learning opportunities and student choice are present in classrooms student attendance increases and disruptions decrease (Robinson, 2011). This type of environment is also important to create for adults in the organization. Teachers are more likely to be engaged in the learning during professional development when the content is meaningful and relevant to their position. Distractions like checking email, sidebar conversations, and grading papers occur when the quality of teaching and learning is low for teachers. Leaders need to make sure that emotionally safe environments are in place for teachers by attending to their learning needs and providing a place where they are challenged to improve practice.

Do This

Be consistent.

Consistency doesn't mean a checklist mentality or religiously following a rigid process. There is comfort in structure because it promotes transparency; however, relying only on this does not account for the complexities of human nature and the organization. What leaders need to do is develop a mindset that allows for flexibility within structure; the authors call this being nimbly consistent. For example consistency with student discipline would include rapid response times, a problem-solving approach, and transparency. The "nimbleness" comes in dealing with individual students based on their needs. Being nimbly consistent means respecting the structure but not allowing it to dictate practice. Sustainability occurs when the structure becomes the vehicle for learning and applying, not the destination. Far too many times teachers and principals fall prey to working through the process or structure without understanding the context, which leads to disengagement. Effective leaders are able to modify or adapt processes and procedures to meet learning needs for themselves and those they serve.

Consistency and predictability are important aspects of building trust. Bryk and Schneider (2002) measured trust in schools and concluded school improvement is impossible without an underlying facet of trust. Schools with high levels of trust are more likely to improve in reading and mathematics than those schools with very low levels of trust. This foundation creates the moral fabric in which teachers, parents, and students can predict the actions of school leaders and trust that safety and order are maintained. When teachers and principals are empowered

36

and feel supported, conflicts can be resolved more quickly. Trust is established through consistency. It predicts how relationships in the school environment are built and nurtured. Developing these relationships improves teaching, learning, and student achievement.

Not That

Waste people's time.

Collaboration is key for successful school improvement efforts. However, when collaborative opportunities are not guided by a clear agenda, members lack interest or conversations are not focused; it wastes precious time and leaves a bad impression. Leaders should focus on three areas to avoid squandering time. First, agendas and outcomes need to be clear to keep meetings focused and efficient. Second, consolidate messages in order to prevent teachers and principals from getting multiple messages throughout the day. Finally, create norms for working together in order not to stray from the agenda with personal stories and interruptions.

Invitational Environment

The physical environment is a tangible artifact that communicates volumes about the learning environment in the school. Leaders have significant control over this environment and need to intentionally tend to it so that spaces are created that invite students to learn. An invitational environment fosters learning. Students spend the majority of their waking day in the school setting so the environment should welcome students and serve as a vehicle for learning. Leaders can organize the environment so it directly influences instruction to invite, inspire, and buoy student learning (Tomlinson, 2002). The fundamental purpose is to create an environment of educational excellence and invitation. The physical environment provides an opportunity to illustrate values, purpose, and pride. These aspects work to motivate staff and students (Peterson & Deal, 2009).

An invitational environment is much more than paint, plants, lamps, and applying inspirational quotes on the walls of the hallway. An invitational setting helps establish tradition. Symbols such as mascots, colors, and songs promote a sense of pride or brand. Displays of student work, banners, and achievements communicate values. Soft comfortable seating invites students and staff to relax and have conversations and shows that collaboration is an important aspect in learning. Artwork, furniture, quotes, and student murals specific to the identity of the age group and school should be an integral part of the building. The school's environment dictates if students and adults feel safe and welcomed.

Do This

Be clear about what you value.

Read the walls: what do they say? Is there a sense that learning is first and excellence is valued? Do the walls reflect the mission of the school? The things we display tell a story and illustrate what matters in the organization. The physical environment should support the purpose of the school, clearly communicating the significant work of the organization. Drab walls, disorganized work areas, and dated posters or sayings do not reflect the unique personality of the students and staff in the school nor do they inspire. Using student work to convey purpose helps students see their contribution to the system. Students and staff must understand that they are cared for and safe. The physical environment plays an important role in making this happen.

Not That

Ignore what matters.

Refusing to notice or intentionally disregarding factors that influence culture has a significant effect on the organization. Culture is a fabric patterned by norms, attitudes, beliefs, behaviors, values, ceremonies, traditions, and myths that are the core of the organization (Barth, 2002). Ignoring any of these threads can convey a message that the leader lacks empathy, and could inadvertently foster toxicity. The perceptions of staff and students are personal; so it's critical that leaders have a pulse on these attitudes and respond positively when necessary. Small things matter. In places where culture is ignored, minute things like the schedule for cleaning out the staff refrigerator can cause major conflicts.

Upholding the ideals associated with this commitment can be daunting, especially when confronted with difficult behaviors. A process called clipboard discipline is shared as an example of the commitment in action at the school level. Shifting a culture at a system level is also very challenging. One district's focus on student displays of work and writing is shared as an example on how to shift the culture and live by this commitment.

Building Level Commitment in Action: Clipboard Discipline

The Issue

The data in the 6th–8th grades, in the school of 950 students, was overwhelming. Approximately 250 discipline incidents were occurring monthly in the school where 75 percent of students were on free or reduced lunch. Secretaries reported that it wasn't uncommon for 20–25 students to be lined up in the office waiting to see an administrator. Students were not only sitting in the office, but could also frequently be found sitting at desks in hallways. While the administrator would have liked to ferret out the root causes for these referrals the sheer volume made it difficult and communicated very clearly that too many students were losing out on valuable instructional time. In order to turn the tide, the leader knew that (a) teachers needed support in order to deal with student behaviors; (b) students needed support in order to learn how to act appropriately; and (c) improvements in student achievement would not occur until the school was safe and orderly.

The Response

The principal developed a system called "clipboard discipline." The purpose was to avoid removing students from the learning environment and to solve the issue where the problem occurred (at the door of the classroom), thus protecting instructional time. In clipboard discipline the administrator meets the student at the classroom door with clipboard in hand so problem solving can occur. The key is to respond to student needs immediately and then collaboratively problem-solve a solution that leads to action (change in student behavior). This process often takes less than 5 minutes and is done privately outside the classroom door. There are several advantages to meeting at the classroom door. First, it protects instructional time; second, there is no miscommunication with the teacher about actions taken by administration; and finally, it models for the teacher how to problem-solve difficult behavior issues.

Before arriving at the classroom door the administrator reviews the information sent with the notification for help. The administrator does three things upon arriving at the classroom door. First, they listen to the child's point of view; second, they problem-solve; and finally they negotiate a solution. An actual clipboard may be used or it may be an iPad, computer, or some other device. The point is that the administrator is working with the student within 5–10 minutes of notification. The point of the response it to determine if a consequence is necessary and what would be most effective in curbing the student's negative behaviors in the future. Principals should consider progressive measures that are natural and will remind the child that the behavior will not be tolerated in this environment.

Critical Features of Clipboard Discipline

● Identify non-negotiable behaviors (students and staff): In order to get started with clipboard discipline a list of non-negotiable behaviors from students, teachers, and guests in the school needs to be in place. The non-negotiable list consists of behaviors that will not be tolerated in the school. Establishing these upfront with students and teachers helps clarify and raise expectations.

- Maintain teacher authority: When teachers send misbehaving students out of the classroom to be disciplined by another adult in the building it subtly undermines the teacher's authority, communicating that they can't handle the problem. One of the critical features of clipboard discipline is to help teachers keep their "power." A teacher notifies administration that they need help either in the form of a consultation or a discipline referral. A consultation is when the teacher needs help with a student who may be exhibiting behaviors that are not a violation of the school's code of conduct, but are getting in the way of learning. A consultation is designed to help the teacher and student work through the issue and may or may not result in a consequence to the student. A discipline referral is defined as a clear violation of the code of conduct and requires a consequence (e.g., cursing out teacher).

- Identify a philosophy that aligns to the school's mission: There are a plethora of instructional discipline resources and programs available to school administrators. The leader needs to collaboratively settle on a research-based foundation. It isn't a specific method that makes clipboard discipline a success; it's the commitment and alignment to the specific mission and needs of the building that is critical.

- Provide ongoing professional development: A variety of approaches to learning the system are necessary. Multimedia presentations that include video, input, reflection (individual or small group), and case studies, presented two to three times monthly during the first year of implementation, are necessary. Without ongoing professional development and training in using the process, clipboard discipline will not work. This approach is not so much about the "clipboard" as it is about instructing all staff and students on how to problem-solve issues. Actual examples of referrals serve as the cornerstone of professional development and allow teachers to brainstorm possible solutions to the common issues occurring in the school.

The Results

Discipline referrals fell from over 2800 to 1150 in the first year. This was a 59 percent decrease from the previous year. In a building whose population is nearly 1000 students this equates to approximately six referrals per day. During the second year of implementation, referrals dropped to 832, equating to 4.2 referrals per day. The third year referrals dropped to 745 with 4.1 per day. The entire environment experienced a dramatic calming. Parent, staff, and student survey results indicated a perception of increased safety, consistent administration of the code of conduct, and that students were treated with respect. One teacher's quote said it all: "I enjoy coming to work again, and we have control of our school."

District Level Commitment in Action: Creating a Culture Focused on Learning

The Issue

The headline was not pretty. Lowest graduation rate in the state. With a 67 percent free or reduced lunch rate and a high dropout rate, the new district leadership knew that they had challenges ahead, but the headline said it all. These results were not due to a lack of effort by the teachers and administrators in the district. Building level administrators were extremely committed to the students and parents, as evidenced by the long hours they spent at school and a series of initiatives implemented aimed at improving achievement. These initiatives were typically driven by a state mandate and were generically implemented across the district with artificial benchmarks and heavy reporting requirements. For example, every teacher must use Strategy X five times each week and fill out a log stating when the strategy was used.

Initial walkthroughs in schools and classrooms by the new Assistant Superintendent, however, revealed less than ideal learning environments. Students were disengaged and classrooms and office areas were disorganized and cluttered. Teachers' workspace in the classroom, frequently referred to as teacher forts, took up large spaces, with stacks of papers and books lining the desk and floor. Expectations for students were low, as evidenced by the preponderance of coloring, cutting, and pasting that had infiltrated the K-12 district curriculum. The first step was to help building leadership understand that the environments and expectations in their schools needed to change. The challenge was to do this in a way that honored the hard work that had occurred prior to the new leader coming on board, yet creating a sense of urgency in the leaders so they understood how imperative it was to improve practice.

The Response

Critical to getting the students to stay in school until they graduated was making sure the schools were places that students wanted to attend. This called for a two-pronged approach: creating welcoming student-centered environments, and addressing the academic rigor in classrooms.

In order to develop a student-centered environment one of the first actions of the Assistant Superintendent was to make sure that principal meetings were redesigned to focus on professional learning. One feature of this time together was to engage in book studies that addressed the importance of the school environment, both how it was organized and the language adults used with students. Coupled with this focus was a field trip to a district in a neighboring state that was an exemplar for the welcoming student-centered settings that the district wanted to create. The district had similar demographics, but high levels of student achievement and graduation rates, providing a much-needed model for school leaders. Being able to see live and in person what this district was doing for a population similar to their students created a much-needed renewed sense of purpose and vision for leaders to create back in their schools.

A focus on writing as a response to reading and thinking was initiated in order to begin the difficult work of increasing academic rigor in the district. The state assessment was entirely a multiple-choice exam so using the writing process and writing on demand had decreased dramatically over the previous years. Writing is the litmus test for thinking, so to help all teachers learn how to help students write across the curriculum a two-year focus was placed on making sure that students had opportunities to write and reflect, but also learn how to improve their writing through conferring and the use of common rubrics.

In an effort to help leaders continually monitor the academic rigor in their classrooms a focus was placed on student displays of work. Principals learned about the qualities and purpose of good displays and look fors were created so all principals could deepen their understanding and a common framework could be developed. The Assistant Superintendent conducted walkthroughs with a keen focus on examining these displays in light of writing. During the first year of these walkthroughs, when children were asked why they did an assignment or what they had learned, it wasn't uncommon to hear answers focused on the arts and crafts nature of the work. Students could be heard saying things like, "It's all about the coloring," or "I did well because my paper is neat." The push for asking students to write in response to reading and thinking quickly helped to uncover this misplaced focus and helped create the sense of urgency in building leaders who wanted more for their students. Discussion with building principals after these visits focused on what was learned from the student work regarding the level of academic rigor in the building, and what were the next steps needed for improvement.

The Results

The most immediate and important result was a dramatic change in discussions about teaching and learning. Discussions were shifting from a focus on inputs (every teacher must use Strategy X) to outputs (what impact does the teaching have on student learning?). Teachers and administrators were placing more value on writing and using this information to help inform instruction. Teacher forts were replaced with a small workspace in the corner of the room, and classrooms were being organized to create spaces where students could work collaboratively and in comfort. While these changes did not result in seismic shifts in student achievement, they created the foothold for the more arduous work ahead in curriculum development and instructional pedagogy. This work helped leaders to make a ruthless analysis of reality so that a shift in culture could occur. Graduation rates improved and the district continually improved academic performance. Getting the leaders and teachers to understand that students needed something different was an important first step.

References

Barth, R. (2002). The culture builder. *Educational Leadership*, 59 (8), 6–11.

Bryk, A. S., & Schneider, B. (2002). *Trust in schools: A core resource for improvement.* New York: Russell Sage Foundation.

Chenoweth, K., & Theokas, C. (2011). *Getting it done: Leading academic success in unexpected schools.* Cambridge, MA: Harvard Education Press.

Fisher, D., & Frey, N. (2012). *How to create a culture of achievement in your school and classroom.* Alexandria, VA: ASCD.

Fullan, M. (2014). *The principal: Three keys to maximizing impact.* San Francisco, CA: Jossey-Bass.

Peterson, K., & Deal, T. (2009). *Shaping school culture: Pitfalls, paradoxes, and promises.* San Francisco, CA: Jossey-Bass.

Robinson, V. M. (2011). *Student centered leadership.* San Francisco, CA: Jossey-Bass.

Sinek, S. (2009). *Start with why.* New York: Penguin Group.

Tomlinson, C. A. (2002). Invitations to learn. *Educational Leadership, 60* (1), 6–10.

Use of a Growth Mindset to Develop and Enhance Professional Capital

Remember that children, marriages, and flower gardens reflect the kind of care they get.

H. Jackson Brown, Jr.

The whole premise of gardening is growth. Gardeners understand that the challenge in developing a beautiful garden lies in having all plants grow. Gardeners aren't satisfied if only half of their garden blooms; they want the entire garden to grow. All plants require watering, weeding, fertilizing, and sun, but the amounts vary depending on needs. The amount of care and feeding required for growth is contingent upon the plant. A seedling needs more attention than a plant that has already developed roots. In order for some plants to grow strong and tall they will need a trellis; others may need to stay low to the ground so beds should be built accordingly. Tending to a garden requires vigilance so that the right supports are in place at the appropriate time during the growing season. Plants left unattended may thrive for a while, but eventually will die on the vine. The thrill of gardening happens when plants come to fruition. Successful gardeners are diligent in providing the care that each plant needs; they understand that without this the garden will not grow.

It is not uncommon for leaders to use the maxim "schools are a people business" to communicate how much they care for and respect their staff. Think of how audacious it would be for a gardener to say, "gardening is a plant business." While plants are essential, it is their development that matters. Gardeners show their respect for the land and their plants by tending to them on a regular basis. Gardening is about growth, and so should be the work in schools and school systems. Schools are a growth business;

teachers' business is to grow students, principals' business is to grow teachers, and central office's business is to grow principals. Growth doesn't happen in a vacuum; it requires deliberate attention and focus. Educational leaders must start with the same premise as the gardener. This requires a growth mindset (Dweck, 2006).

People with a growth mindset, according to Dweck's research, believe that their most basic abilities (i.e., intelligence, talent) can be improved through hard work and dedication, in contrast to those with a fixed mindset who believe these abilities are set and can't be developed. A growth mindset creates a love of learning and a resilience that leads to greater and greater accomplishments. Educational leaders need to believe that all teachers and principals in a school or system have the potential to develop if given the right conditions. Neglecting to support staff with the day-to-day demands of helping students learn sends the message that the leader doesn't care and can reinforce a fixed mindset. A fixed mindset is exhibited when leaders fail to consistently observe and provide feedback, when they treat evaluation as an event, and have a checklist mentality to school improvement.

Believing that all individuals have the potential to polish their practice requires school leaders to provide the right conditions for growth. Under the guise of autonomy many leaders use a hands-off approach because they feel that this is effective; however, this implies that the teacher has peaked. Growth happens along a continuum. Leaders must think deeply about the learning needs of the organization and then develop an environment that addresses learning and lifts performance.

Commitment as Development of Professional Capital—Human Capital

Human capital is the third dimension that makes up professional capital. To understand human capital one must understand the interconnectedness between human and social capital. Human capital is about talent or the quality of the individual, while social capital focuses on the group (Hargreaves & Fullan, 2012). A strong relationship must exist in a school or a system between social and human capital. Human capital increases when there is high social capital in an organization. Individuals grow when they interact and develop relationships within a group. However, if the focus is on only developing individual talent then social capital does not increase. Focusing on social capital will increase the capacity of the individual while also increasing group capacity. The symbiotic nature of this relationship requires a leader to tend to both and is one of the reasons why a commitment to a healthy culture, as described in Chapter 3, is paramount to this work. Developing human capital is critical; the quality of the teacher and leader in a school has been proven time and time again to have a major influence on student achievement (Leithwood, Day, Sammons, Harris, & Hopkins, 2006; Marzano, 2003). How human capital is developed, however, must shift from a singular focus on the individual and move to a broader focus on the group, with an eye on individual growth and development within this setting. The work of developing human capital flows from the skills and knowledge gained through collaborative learning experiences.

Leaders who commit to enhancing development through the use of a growth mindset have a keen understanding of the relationship between human and social capital. They use the learning that occurs during collaborative work to support individual growth. Leaders who commit to this work spend as much time, if not more, making sure that the structures and composition of the group will help and support the learning of the individual. When a staff member's performance is not at desired levels, they examine both group interactions and dynamics as well as individual skills and knowledge. They organize learning in the school for optimal growth for all and differentiate supervision practices to meet individual needs.

Indicators of Critical Concepts and Commitment in Practice

Committing to a growth mindset requires the leader to look at supervision in a different light. It requires a vow to take actions that cultivate growth rather than focusing on individual cures. There are three critical concepts that a leader who is committed to using a growth mindset to develop professional capital must grasp. They are as follows:

- **Collaborative inquiry** is key to growth.
- Improvement involves addressing both **content and process learning**.
- **Feedback** is vital for growth.

Collaborative Inquiry

It has long been established that collaboration works. Schools where teachers collaborate on an ongoing basis outperform schools where collaboration doesn't exist (Rosenholtz, 1985; Newmann & Wehlage, 1995; McLaughlin & Talbert, 2001; Leana, 2011). However, it has also been proven that not all efforts at collaboration are created equal (Little, 1990). A taken-for-granted assumption by many leaders is that if they put people in teams and identify times for them to meet, collaboration will occur and results will improve. The reality is much harsher; collaboration that works requires planning and an inquiry stance. It requires leaders to thoughtfully and deliberately put teams together, considering individuals' strengths while also setting up structures and processes that allow teams to pose questions, hypothesize answers, and use evidence to support or show fallibility of claims.

The process of collaborative inquiry requires teachers and leaders to assess and modify their pre-conceived notions of teaching and learning practices by coming together to solve problems using evidence. The hallmark of an inquiry-based culture is when teams are adept at using information and reasoning to determine next steps even when it challenges pre-existing beliefs. This is when rich learning occurs. Learning is the acquisition of skills and knowledge through study and experience. Implicit in this definition is action; learning requires synthesizing new information and comparing to existing understanding in order to make meaning. Teachers and principals need multiple opportunities to examine the impact of instructional practices, question their efficiency, discuss implications, and adjust thinking in order to learn and grow. A culture of collaborative inquiry provides the learning platform needed to do this work.

Do This

Nurture collective responsibility.

Collective responsibility means having a sense of responsibility for both one's own actions and students and the actions of colleagues and other students in the school or system (Newmann, 1994). Inspiring collective responsibility requires the leader to create conditions that help everyone in the organization realize how individual efforts are mutually supportive of collective efforts. An "all for one, one for all" attitude prevails in organizations with high collective responsibility. Teachers and leaders who take collective responsibility understand that helping colleagues work through a problem of practice, even when it isn't an immediate problem for them personally, helps them hone their skills and gain confidence. They understand that two heads are better than one, and when they are struggling with a problem the team can be counted on to assist them with identifying solutions.

Central to developing a culture of collective responsibility is using evidence for improvement (Robinson, 2014). While data seems to be abundant in schools today, the key here is to identify and use data that helps inform daily practice. The preponderance of data used during collaborative inquiry must come from student work. This doesn't mean that district and high stakes state assessment data aren't useful, because they are; however, these data points serve as markers or destinations along the learning journey. While it is important to mark progress in this way to determine if headed in the right direction, it is critical to make sure that the wheels are properly aligned and on the road at all times. Common measures developed by the team are a powerful resource that helps to drive day-to-day decision-making. In order for these measures to be useful, teams need a rich understanding of what students need to know and do, an aptitude for identifying ways to figure out if students have learned, the ability to interpret student data, and multiple strategies to understand how to respond when students don't learn. It isn't any wonder then that this can't be done in isolation. This is complex and demanding work and requires all hands on deck. Leaders who make this commitment understand this and create the conditions in the school that support and nurture this work.

Not That

Make assumptions about teams.

There are two faulty assumptions that occur when working in collaborative teams. The first assumption is that staff know how to work in teams and, if they don't, a couple of "trainings" at the beginning of the year will be sufficient to help them learn. This is what Elisa MacDonald (2013) calls the instant coffee approach to leading teams. Just mix in an agenda, a leader, and a few trainings and "poof" you have a team. This approach results in the same richness as an instant cup of coffee. The goal for a leader is to have high functioning, high impact teams. This means that the teams not only work well together, but also their work improves results for students (MacDonald, 2013). Achieving this level of collaborative teaming requires continuous attention to both how the team is functioning and the level of impact. Using team norms, agenda, and protocols helps teams meet shared goals when used consistently. As the opening quote to this chapter communicates, marriages, children, and gardens are a reflection of the care they receive, and so it goes for collaborative teams. In order to grow and develop, teams need a skilled facilitator who can help them navigate the hurdles that are inherent when working together to solve complex problems. This means leaders must be active members of these teams, and while they shouldn't always be leading the team, they do need to make sure that the team has the tools it needs to be productive. Without an ongoing presence at team meetings a leader has a difficult time knowing the level of functioning and would not be able to determine if the composition of the team has the right mix of individuals. Leaders who understand the power of professional capital and are committed to a growth mindset understand that the work in collaborative teams influences individual development. They strategically develop teams to make sure that all teachers will grow from the experience.

The second faulty assumption about teams is that they should all be treated the same. Like the children in our schools, teams don't all start at the same level, nor do they develop at the same rate. Conceptually leaders understand this, but in practice the level of support may look the same for each team if leaders aren't nimbly consistent. Effective leaders scrutinize team dynamics and the context of the work to identify level of functioning, and adjust supports accordingly. Some teams may need more direct engagement and tools while others can function with basic team structures. Leaders with a growth mindset understand that the team's level of functioning isn't fixed and will improve over time given the right reinforcements. Leaders also understand that levels of collaboration may vary within a team depending on the inquiry cycle. As firmly held beliefs get called into question, teams will grapple with developing satisfactory conclusions and need the support of a skilled leader. Even teams that tend to be high impact and are high functioning will struggle at times. Savvy leaders understand this and adjust their levels of support to meet various teams' needs.

Content and Process Learning

To quote Lauren Resnick, "knowledge and thinking must be intimately joined" (1999, p. 40). For students this means that it's impossible to teach thinking in the absence of teaching knowledge. Curriculum must include a commitment to a knowledge core and a high thinking demand so students can actively use knowledge. Basically students need knowledge, think deeply, and apply what they have learned to new situations. For adults leading schools and school systems this same concept holds true. Leaders need to have a strong core in teaching and learning. Core knowledge on teaching requires a leader to understand what students need to know in specific content areas. While a leader can't be an expert in all content areas a deep understanding of what students should know and do in math and literacy is mandatory. Core knowledge on learning requires leaders to understand effective instructional practices. The authors refer to this knowledge as content knowledge. Content knowledge alone isn't enough. Like the student who has a lot of knowledge, but can't apply it to complex situations, leaders who don't understand how to apply content knowledge to improve an organization will not be successful. Leaders need to think deeply about what it takes to move the system forward. This requires what the authors refer to as process knowledge. School leaders need to know content (what) and they need to think about and use structures and processes (how) that allow this content to be implemented at high levels.

Leaders who are committed to a growth mindset to develop professional capital understand that growth will be stymied if both content and process learning aren't addressed. Professional development in schools should help learners become consciously competent, a term developed by Noel Burch in the 1970s that means that an individual knows what to do and knows why what they are doing works. Teachers need to learn about their content and they need to understand what processes and procedures facilitate learning in their classrooms. Principals and central office leaders need opportunities to develop content knowledge and a rich understanding of the processes that work to improve a school or a system.

Do This

Think "and," not "either or."

When planning professional learning experiences, include both content and process learning. This doesn't mean that every learning opportunity requires both, but it does mean that both areas need considerable attention throughout the year. Content learning is typically what is focused on during professional learning with teachers. Incorporating process learning requires the building principal to spend time helping teachers navigate and understand the processes that facilitate learning and/or move a school forward. Process learning in schools helps teachers answer questions such as, "What instructional moves are helping students answer higher level questions?" or "How are you responding when students do not meet the daily learning target?" or "How do we ensure that all staff use Strategy X?" At the district level, process learning helps principals answer such questions as, "What is the structure for learning teams and what should teams be doing during team time?", "How do we use protocols to help with analysis of student work?", or "How is professional development aligned to a school improvement plan?" Finding the right balance between content and process can be challenging, but without an "and" stance gains in student achievement can't be sustained or replicated.

Not That

Confuse implementation for understanding.

Schools and school systems are full of good soldiers. Good soldiers are those people that support the district or school by implementing initiatives even when they don't understand the value or purpose in doing so. Having a system full of good soldiers is not entirely a bad thing, as Fullan has taught us practice comes before belief (Fullan, 2011). The problem with a preponderance of people with this attitude is that many times their compliance masks misconceptions they have and if left unchecked over time fosters resentment and confusion. Ann was feeling pretty puffed up one year after she had trained principals on how to develop their school improvement and professional development plan. Overall the plans that were turned in were aligned and focused, so she was taken off guard when she walked into one school to observe a professional learning session and the content had nothing to do with the strategies outlined in the plan. In her conversation with the principal after the session Ann realized it wasn't because the principal was trying to be a free agent; the principal didn't understand the relationship between the plan and staff learning. Checking for understanding through face-to-face discussions and frequent observations is critical in order to determine if content and process learning is hitting the mark.

Feedback

Feedback is the fertilizer of professional learning. It is what helps nurture and accelerate growth. In all walks of life, be it medicine, professional sports, or the fitness industry, feedback is a welcome and vital component used to improve practice. Unfortunately in education feedback has been viewed negatively due to its use or misuse with traditional teacher appraisal systems. The feedback associated with this process is evaluative in the sense that it is used to make judgments about how weak or strong a teacher or leader might be. It is not the purpose of this book to discuss formal appraisal systems; it is clear that many of them need to be overhauled. The purpose here is to help leaders see and use feedback as a vehicle for growth. The goal of supervisory feedback is to help individuals become consciously competent so practice can improve. Effective feedback should help promote self-awareness and serve as that voice in a person's head that has them constantly thinking and reflecting on how to advance performance.

Feedback should be designed so it can be acted upon, which requires it to be treated more as a cycle rather than a "one and done." Frequent observations with accompanying feedback are necessary so a culture of continuous learning can be developed. When leaders offer feedback with the purpose of growth and are transparent in the use of feedback, collaborative cultures flourish (Fullan, 2014). Growth occurs when there are high expectations and high support. Feedback, when used as described in Section II, provides both.

Do This

Make providing feedback for growth a priority.

Two issues can hinder a leader from using the feedback cycle for improvement. The first is time. Prominent importance must be placed on conducting observations and providing feedback in order for this practice to become a habit. A leader needs to organize their day so observations take precedence over office work or other managerial tasks. Leaders must make a conscious effort to schedule portions of their day, every day, for observations and feedback. This is the real work of leading teaching and learning and principals and central office staff should not be bashful or feel guilty about making this a priority. We wouldn't want to go to a doctor who spent the majority of his/her time filling out charts; we want a doctor who engages in the practice of medicine by working with patients. We want and need principals who spend the majority of their time working with teachers to improve learning, and we need central office administrators who spend the majority of their time working with principals to improve their practice.

Another hurdle to making feedback a priority for leaders is the inability to focus or be specific. Unfortunately many educational leadership programs and observation tools that accompany teacher appraisal systems have leaders providing feedback on every aspect of an observation. This is ineffective because it doesn't change practice, the goal of feedback. Science and experience have taught us that it is impossible to try to improve too many things at once. In order to maximize development, feedback needs to be focused on one thing.

Frequent feedback given in small chunks over time has a greater impact on performance than a volume of feedback given infrequently (Bambrick-Santoyo, 2012). Leaders need to home in on one item at a time, provide feedback, and support to help ensure that feedback is used for improvement.

Not That

Rely only on written feedback.

While written feedback in the form of notes and emails is powerful, face-to-face feedback provides the biggest bang for the buck (Bambrick-Santoyo, 2012; Marshall, 2013). The power in face-to-face feedback is that it allows the leader to ask probing questions. Asking probing questions is effective because it helps the giver of the feedback complete their diagnosis regarding the practice and it allows the receiver of the feedback to do some thinking. The goal of feedback is to change practice. If an individual isn't allowed to do the thinking, learning won't be internalized. When individuals participate in feedback discussions and are asked to think about their practice they are more likely to own the learning and subsequently adjust practice.

A growth mindset requires a leader to commit to achievement; reaching or meeting a desired outcome. Two examples of what types of achievement can occur when leading with a growth mindset follow. The first example shares how a building's collaborative processes evolved. Structuring opportunities for principal growth will be shared as an example of a district practice that exemplifies this commitment.

Building Level Commitment in Action: Collaboration that Works

The Issue

Significant increases in student achievement cannot occur overnight or through the talents of one individual. Faced with reorganization due to No Child Left Behind sanctions, one principal took over a school where less than 50 percent of students were proficient in reading and math on state assessments. While teaming and common plan times were in place, teachers were asked to raise achievement by following a seventy-page school improvement plan. Strategies were provided for every content area and every teacher worked within a silo and collaborated only when events needed to be organized. While team time was scheduled, it was up to the purview of the teachers on the team how this time was utilized. Teachers worked hard but their direction was uncharted and their results were sporadic. Teachers did not have a working knowledge of how to improve instruction so that it impacted learning. The staff was comprised of dedicated professionals who would follow where led even when the roadmap was murky. The leader knew the direction forward was with a "skinny" school improvement plan, and a focus on development of the staff. It was time to put the learning in PLC (Fullan 2009).

The Response

The first step in making the change occur was to develop the capacity among formal and informal leaders in the building. A leadership team was formed and retreats were scheduled to provide professional development in the area of school improvement and to develop teacher leaders. The principal explained the school improvement process using analogies and practical examples that provided authentic application. This team served as the information hub and helped to make the information go viral throughout the school. Team members were trusted by staff to provide real answers and to help explain initiatives.

The second step, which happened simultaneously with the first step, was to structure collaborative learning. Three foundational processes

58

needed to be put in place to make sure that collaborative teaming resulted in rich learning and changed student outcomes. First, a consistent schedule was developed so teachers would meet on a regular basis; teams were required to meet three times a week. Administrators were active participants at these meetings. Next, teachers needed a predictable structure for team learning time. This structure consisted of a warm-up (grows and glows), a guiding question to promote discourse around backward planning, student work, or responding to student needs, and finally meetings ended with reflection on learning and following norms. The final and most important component was to foster and prompt discourse on the guiding questions by all members of the team. This happened through the use of effective tools such as protocols, backward planners, data analysis sheets, and other resources that supported uncovering the answers to the guiding questions. Appendix A provides an example of a structured agenda. Appendix B provides the template for a backward planner. Many times this meant that the collaborative meetings became mini workshops with staff learning a new strategy or approach that would help meet their students' particular learning needs.

The Results

Teachers were empowered in making instructional decisions that positively affected their classroom and students. The tighter alignment on the curriculum and use of a backward plan were reflected in consistent implementation across the grade level. The collaboration of the team created a sense of shared effort in accomplishing goals. Planning and analysis of assessment were less overwhelming for teachers because there were others who shared in the responsibility. Teachers were seen providing feedback to one another as a result of consistent use of a protocol. Trust among peers was obvious and respect for ideas was valued. Most importantly, the use of this system of collaborative support and professional development resulted in a 14 percent increase in achievement within two school years. The once failing school had turned the tide and was not turning back.

District Level Commitment in Action: Leveraging Learning for Leaders

The Issue

With the advent of new district leadership, principals' meetings in a mid-sized urban district were reorganized with a focus on professional learning. Nuts and bolts items were sent in a weekly communication so that time spent in face-to-face meetings with building leaders was spent discussing and learning about relevant issues related to leading teaching and learning. This was a welcome shift for principals who prior to this time were used to "sit and get" meetings where a variety of district administrators paraded in and out sharing the latest urgent deadline or process. However, even though topics were limited to two learning outcomes (one on process and one on content) that had a direct bearing on the work of the principal, the meetings continued to be delivered in a traditional vein. The Assistant Superintendent presented information via PowerPoint and while principals had time to discuss new learning in small groups, this drove the topics and content. While the whole group professional learning was helping principals gain new skills, it was not meeting everyone's needs. Supervisory walk-throughs conducted by the Assistant Superintendent and student achievement scores indicated that principals were at varying stages in regard to understanding and using school improvement processes and leading instruction. After a couple of years of this one-dimensional approach, building leaders asked for and district leaders understood that a richer process was needed.

The Response

A layered approach was needed if all principals' learning needs were going to be met. Whole group professional development sessions continued to be held monthly, but instead of this time being completely dominated by content deemed appropriate at the district level, principals were put into learning teams and provided time each meeting to pursue learning based on their areas of focus for their school improvement plan. For example, if several buildings were using formative assessment as an improvement strategy these principals would form a learning team for the year. The team would determine what question would lead their inquiry on this topic. District level administrators joined teams and served as a member partnering in the learning, not driving the learning.

Another shift that was made was the implementation of cluster visits. Cluster visits provided building leaders with an opportunity to observe a practice or process being implemented at high levels. These small group meetings lasted one hour and consisted of three or four principals observing the practice in a school and then debriefing the experience. Principals determined which cluster visit they wanted to attend based on their building school improvement needs. When a new literacy model that used a workshop model was being implemented, principals had a choice on whether they needed to observe mini lessons, conferring, guided practice, or sharing.

Finally, principals received ongoing support and feedback through one-on-one visits with district supervisors. These meetings provided the building principal with a chance to discuss the issues in their school with a knowledgeable other who helped problem-solve and support needs. The frequency of these visits was based on the needs of the schools and the leader. All buildings received a visit at least monthly, while some received visits on a weekly basis.

The Results

Principals had more control of their own learning, empowering them to dig deeper into topics based on the context of their school. They developed richer relationships with their colleagues through the ongoing commitment to learning from each other both through cluster visits and monthly learning teams. Lateral capacity increased as leaders shared and worked together to problem-solve through similar struggles. Central office leaders' learning also multiplied as they had opportunities to learn from and respond to individual principals' needs. Working in small groups throughout the year helped these leaders understand the hurdles associated with implementing new learning and gave them the opportunity to tailor support to the individual.

References

Bambrick-Santoyo, P. (2012). *Leverage leadership: A practical guide to building exceptional schools.* San Francisco, CA: Jossey-Bass.

Dweck, C. (2006). *Mindset: The new psychology of success.* New York: Random House.

Fullan, M. (2009). *Motion leadership: The skinny on becoming change savvy.* Thousand Oaks, CA: Corwin Press.

Fullan, M. (2011). *The six secrets of change: What the best leaders do to help their organizations survive and thrive.* San Francisco, CA: Jossey-Bass.

Fullan, M. (2014). *The principal: Three keys to maximizing impact.* San Francisco, CA: Jossey-Bass.

Hargreaves, A., & Fullan, M. (2012). *Professional capital: Transforming teaching in every school.* New York: Teachers College Press & Toronto: Ontario Principals Council.

Leana, C. R. (2011, Fall). The missing link in school reform. *Stanford Social Innovation Review.* http://ssir.org/articles/entry/the_missing_link_in_school_reform/

Leithwood, K., Day, C., Sammons, P., Harris, A., & Hopkins, D. (2006). *Seven strong claims about successful school leadership.* Nottingham: National College for School Leadership/Department of Education and Skills.

Little, J. W. (1990). The persistence of privacy: Autonomy and initiative in teachers' professional relations. *Teachers College Record, 91* (4), 509–536.

MacDonald, E. B. (2013). *The skillful team leader: A resource for overcoming hurdles to professional learning for student achievement.* Thousand Oaks, CA: Corwin Press.

McLaughlin, M., & Talbert, J. (2001). *Professional communities and the work of high school teaching.* Chicago, IL: University of Chicago Press.

Marshall, K. (2013). *Rethinking teacher supervision and evaluation: How to work smart, build collaboration, and close the achievement gap,* 2nd ed. San Francisco, CA: Jossey-Bass.

Marzano, R. J. (2003). *What works in schools: Translating research into action.* Alexandria, VA: ASCD.

Newmann, F. (1994). *School-wide professional community: Issues in restructuring schools* (Issue Report no. 6). Madison, WI: Center on Organization and Restructuring.

Newmann, F. M., & Wehlage, G. (1995). *Successful school restructuring.* Madison, WI: Center on Organization and Restructuring.

Resnick, L. B. (1999, June). Making America smarter. *Education Week, 40* (18), 38–40.

Robinson, V. M. J. (2014). *Student-centered leadership.* Hoboken, NJ: Jossey-Bass.

Rosenholtz, J. (1985, May). Effective schools: Interpreting the evidence. *American Journal of Education, 93* (3), 352–388.

II

Seasons

Working the Field to Get Higher Results

Fall

Starting the Year with Clarity and Focus

Fertilizer does no good in a heap, but a little spread around works miracles all over.

Richard Brinsley Sheridan

Gardening is about timing and tools. Knowing when and how to plant determines the success of the harvest. Veteran gardeners know that different seeds have different growing seasons, and plant accordingly. They understand that there is a window of opportunity when it comes to planting and if it is lost they have to wait for the season to cycle around again. Armed with this information they gather their tools and get to work.

A gardener would never attempt the laborious process of planting a garden without the right tools. Having and using the proper tools is not a luxury, but a necessity. Without a hoe or a power tiller it is easy to see how difficult planting would be and why a gardener may get frustrated and give up. The frustration that many administrators face with reform efforts can be reduced by engaging in certain behaviors and using the power tools for school improvement (Mooney & Mausbach, 2008). The first time a new tool is used, whether it is a rototiller or look fors, may cause discomfort, but eventually, after *repeated* use, the benefits of using the tool become clear. Tools help the gardener define the garden and make it a reality.

Fall is an extremely busy and critical time for a school leader. The beginning of a new school year is a fertile time when the seeds of school improvement must be planted. If the leader allows the myriad of details that accompany a new school year to divert their attention then a golden opportunity is missed and school improvement efforts may stall. During this time of year it is essential for leaders to use the tools of school improvement.

The "have to dos" during the fall include using important tools. They are:

- Have to Do: Engage staff in developing/revising a plan for improvement.
- Have to Do: Collaboratively develop look fors.
- Have to Do: Differentiate supervision for staff.

Have to Do: Engage Staff in Developing/ Revising a Plan for Improvement

Fullan's (2009) idea of "skinny," boiling down the change into the smallest number of key high yield factors that have impact on learning, is how the authors approach the development and revision of school improvement plans. The goal of the school improvement plan is to effect change in the system, and in order to increase the speed of the change and have large-scale reform (whole school or whole district) leaders must follow the concept of "simplexity" (Kluger, 2009). "Simplexity" means the plans are less than complex, but not overly simple.

In order to achieve simplexity, attention must be given to using clear and deliberate language. Schools and school systems are highly compartmentalized, both by physical and organizational design. Teachers in the science wing may rarely interact with the fine arts wing, not only because they are physically separated, but because the school schedule does not allow for common planning or lunch times. This isolation hampers reform efforts and adds to confusion or disengagement. One of the first steps in engaging staff in the development or revision of the school's plan is to use common language consistently. The following questions and language help create shared meaning and clarity for leaders and their teams.

- Where are we going? (answer becomes goals)
- What do we need to do to get there? (answer becomes strategies)
- How do we get the work done? (answer becomes action steps and professional development plan)

Goals

> *Goal setting works because it forces decisions about relative importance—about what is more important in this context, at this time, than all the other important things.*
>
> Viviane Robinson

Sometimes the hardest part about being a school leader is learning to say no to the myriad of initiatives in today's competitive environment. Schools' fears about being publicly shamed by being on "the list" result in leaders looking for a quick fix. Like the lady in the diner in the infamous scene in *When Harry Met Sally*, school leaders look to other districts and say, "I'll have what they're having," even if it isn't right for their district or school. Setting goals, as Viviane Robinson (2014) so eloquently puts it, can help leaders resist these urges and focus on what matters most for their school/district.

There are many acceptable methods for writing goals. The research on PLCs provides many examples of how to develop specific, measurable, attainable, results-oriented and time-bound (SMART) goals with teams (Dufour, Dufour, Eaker, & Many, 2012). The skinny when it comes to developing SMART goals is to make sure that the statements address behavior, criteria, and conditions. An example of a goal statement that includes behavior, criteria, and conditions is as follows:

> By May 2014, ABC School will improve reading comprehension skills (*behavior*) as evidenced by having 83 percent proficient or advanced (*criteria*) on the state assessment and on the ACT reading subtest (*conditions*).

The importance of including each of these factors in goal setting is shown in Figure 5.1. The problem with goals such as "Increase graduation rates" or "Improve math problem solving" is that a team cannot measure results. One of the biggest culture killers is to engage staff in school reform and then not have any measurable results. Given the energy and focus required to implement a plan, it is educational malpractice to write goals that do not address the three factors. As Rick Stiggins (2014) said, students can hit any target if they know what it is and it holds still; the same holds true for staff.

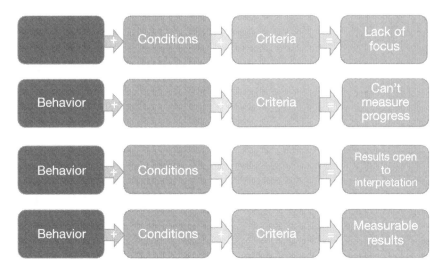

Figure 5.1 Importance of Using Behavior, Conditions, and Criteria
in Goal Setting

Questions for Reflection

Development Stage

- Do the goals include behavior, criteria, and conditions?
- Do the goals address the major issues in the school or system?

Refinement Stage

- Do the goals include behavior, criteria, and conditions?
- What do the results of the goals tell you about your school?
- If the goal was successfully implemented was there a noticeable difference in the school?

Strategies

The term strategy can conjure up many different definitions. When it comes to developing a school improvement plan, strategy is defined as a short-term statement that describes what must be done to meet the goal. While goals focus on the outcomes, strategies are the inputs necessary to achieve desired outcomes. In the authors' experience, identifying high leverage strategies is where many administrators get stuck when planning for improvement. Table 5.1 outlines some of the reasons leaders struggle identifying strategies.

Table 5.1 Pitfalls Teams Make When Identifying Strategies

Pitfall	Example of Pitfall in Practice
Confuse programs with strategies	Implement xyz reading intervention program
Think action steps are strategies	Identify factors that influence student perceptions of their safety at school
Use ambiguous language or buzz words	Differentiate instruction

Consider the implications in focus given strategies A and B in Table 5.2. Strategy A provides a clear focus to teachers about where the school is headed and helps inform the learning that needs to occur. Strategy A invests in people by helping them improve their practice. The driver in strategy B is the resource.

Table 5.2 Goal, Strategy, and Action Step Examples

Goal: By May 2014, ABC School will improve reading comprehension skills as evidenced by having 83 percent proficient or advanced on the state assessment and an increase on the ACT reading subtest.
Strategy A: Implement common reading strategies for each curricular area that will be taught and reinforced during focus lessons.
Strategy B: Implement xyz program.
Action Steps: • Study *Improving Adolescent Literacy* by Fisher and Frey. • Identify focus strategies for each content area. • Develop look fors for reading strategies in each content area.

Strategies are what operationalize the goal, and in order for the goal to be met all staff need to clearly understand what needs to be accomplished. A clearly articulated strategy aids in staff's understanding of the work that lies ahead. Identifying a program as a strategy communicates that meeting the goal is outside of the teacher's influence and all that is necessary is to purchase and implement. While there are many good resources and programs available to teachers, what matters most is the quality of the teacher (Marzano, Pickering, & Pollock, 2001). Commercially developed programs are effective when they are placed in the hands of a competent teacher who knows not only how to use the tool, but why and for which students. Rather than focusing a strategy on a program, a school leader is better served by focusing on people and process. If a leader wants to harness the professional capital (Hargreaves & Fullan, 2012) in the school they must begin to think about improvement strategies in these terms.

Questions for Reflection

Development Stage

- Is the strategy a short-term statement that describes what must be done to meet the goal?
- Do the strategies propose projects that, when accomplished, will lead to part of the goal being completed?
- Will the implementation of the strategies result in improved practices throughout the school or the system?
- Have one to two strategies been identified per goal? (think skinny)

Refinement Stage

- Was there full implementation of the strategy (every child benefited from the innovation)?
- How does the evidence collected of strategy implementation inform next steps?

Action Steps

Action means action. The key to action steps is to make sure that they outline the important steps necessary to getting the strategy implemented throughout the school. Action steps include the activities that will be used and resources purchased so that wide-scale implementation will occur. These steps serve as the school's "to do" list and help keep the leader accountable for the work.

An example of a few action steps aligned to a goal and strategy can be found in Table 5.2. Keeping the concept of simplexity in mind, leaders are encouraged to include the critical steps necessary to get the work done, but not include a laundry list of minutiae. The purpose of a school improvement plan is to provide focus and clarity. If the action steps are getting too long the plan is in danger of not being understood or used. Clarity and focus are the key to writing action steps.

Questions for Reflection

Development Stage

- Do the action steps include action?
- If completed will the action steps lead to implementation of the strategy?
- Are the steps manageable? Can you complete several in one year?

Refinement Stage

- Which actions were completed?
- Are there action steps that need to be refined or deleted?
- Do you need to add action steps given any revisions made to goal or strategy?

Professional Development Plan

Professional development is the engine of school improvement. Professional development makes the plan work, but only if there is tight alignment. Careful attention must be paid to developing a professional development plan based on strategies and action steps. Thus, the professional development plan is typically the last section to be developed in the school improvement plan (SIP).

In order to develop an aligned professional development plan, attention must be paid to both the infrastructure for learning in the school and the content. Figure 5.2 depicts the levels of support necessary. Support comes in layers rather than in tiers, an important distinction that results in multiple support structures depending on the desired level of impact. In other words, one size does not fit all, so a variety of structures must be utilized simultaneously.

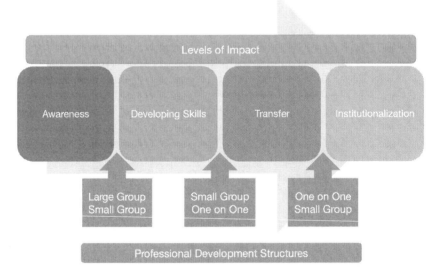

Figure 5.2 Professional Development Structures

A professional development plan should include the name/description of the learning activity, alignment to the strategy, projected dates, resources needed, and evaluation of activities. If a thorough job has been done in identifying action steps for each strategy the professional development plan will emerge naturally. Consolidating professional development into the final section of the overall plan is necessary as it helps serve as a gauge for whether or not the school can actually implement all of the initiatives in the plan.

The professional development plan is fluid, and as principals gather evidence of strategy implementation, observe in classrooms, and analyze student work, adjustments will need to be made. However, without a tentative long-range (one year) plan for professional growth, the learning of teachers can fall prey to the dreaded "activity" trap, treating professional learning as a series of events that are loosely coupled, lack relevance, and have little hope of impacting teaching and learning.

Questions for Reflection

Development Stage

- Does the plan include all of the professional development outlined in the action steps for each strategy?
- Is the professional development plan manageable?
- Does the plan include all of the learning that needs to occur in order for staff to fully implement strategies?
- Do you have the infrastructure in place to provide whole group, small group, and one-on-one learning opportunities?

Refinement Stage

- Did you stay on track with the plan? Why or why not?
- Do you need to change the infrastructure for professional learning in order to ensure deep levels of implementation?
- If changes were made to the strategies and action steps, what impact does that have on the professional learning plan?

Principal Moves

Move 1: Create an Organizational Structure that Enables All Staff to Buy in

In order for all staff to engage in both the development and refinement of the school improvement plan a principal must have structures in place that allow for all staff to systematically provide input and review progress. Many schools have leadership teams in place that address a variety of topics or issues in the school; however, the authors are advocating for a structure designed so the school improvement plan and corresponding professional development plan are the priority for the team's work. Depending on the size of the school, the number of teams will vary, but as a rule of thumb all instructional staff need to be on a school improvement committee. If the plan has three goals, then there should be three teams around each goal. A member from each goal team would also serve on the overall school leadership team. If the school has an extremely large staff, then each goal team needs to make sure that at least one representative from each department or team is on the committee. This ensures that information developed and reviewed during team meetings can be shared throughout the school. The key is to have a structure and then to put the issues of school improvement as the focus of agendas.

Move 2: Utilize Data to Develop/Revise Plan

Chapter 8 shares a process called the Data Consult for summarizing and synthesizing building data. The data portfolio developed during the consult is the impetus for developing and/or revising the school improvement plan. During the fall the principal needs to ensure that they revisit this data to make sure that major issues are addressed in the school improvement plan.

Move 3: Revisit and Revise the Mission

Developing, revising, or revisiting the mission and vision in the fall is critical to establish the fabric for the work of school improvement. Peter Senge (2011) has taught us that vision is everyone's job and is a catalyst that carries staff through celebrations and struggles. A mission and vision along with value and belief statements inspire the staff and remind them of the reasons they do the work. Without a strong vision, beliefs, and values, progress may stall from inefficiency and lack of clarity. The authors spent many years going through the steps of school improvement: writing goals, identifying strategies, implementing action steps, and aligning professional development. Growth occurred but it was gradual and staff didn't consistently understand the "why." It wasn't until the importance of mission and the role it plays in motivating staff was front and center that accelerated gains in achievement occurred. The mission grounds the educational community with the rationale and moral purpose, providing a foundation for the stamina that will be needed as they embark on change; it buoys the staff through the day-to-day challenges.

Writing, sharing, and celebrating the mission is critical; however, it's the reflective questioning and responsive action that helps the leader to eliminate barriers to changing the culture and climate. Refining the mission and reflecting on the core values and beliefs act as a map to navigate change. The leader needs to cultivate the mission by consistently getting staff input and then responding accordingly. Table 5.3 outlines the questions frequently used when working with staff to either develop or revise the mission.

Table 5.3 Questions for Mission Development and Revision

Development Stage
• What is the mission of our school? Why do we exist? • What is the vision of our school? What must we become? • What do we value at our school? How do these guide behaviors? • What are our goals for the year? How will we mark progress? • What are the three most important priorities at our school in order to increase student achievement?
Refinement Stage
• Does the mission of our school match what we say and do? How? • Does the vision of our school meet our aspirations? How? • Do our values guide our behaviors? How? • Do the goals for this year still make sense? • Have the three most important priorities at our school in order to increase student achievement changed?

(Adapted from Dufour, Dufour, Eaker, & Many, 2012)

Central Office Moves

Move 1: Develop/Use Common Template

Central office staff must develop a common template for all principals to use in a system. To be clear, a common template does not mean having the same goals, strategies, and action steps for each school. Each school in a system needs to identify the goals, strategies, and action steps based on their data; however, a common planning template helps with clarity and simplexity by enhancing communication with all district stakeholders. A common format helps other district leaders and board members understand individual buildings' needs and goals, allowing central office staff to differentiate supports. It also aids in identifying common themes so that professional development supports can be provided. Appendix C provides an example of both an expanded template and the one-pager that the authors have used. The one-pager was used with the Board of Education so they could understand the major issues for each school in the system and not be overloaded with information.

Using a common template also aids in reflection and revision. In order to be reflective, practitioner leaders need to reflect both on action and in action. Reflection in action, according to Hargreaves and Fullan (2012), is the ability to walk around a problem while you are in the middle of it. The questions in Table 5.4 help a leader and their teams reflect in the moment, adjusting the plan as necessary. Without a format that organizes the plan into meaningful sections, rich reflection is difficult.

Move 2: Provide Training

As discussed in Chapter 4, one of the critical commitments of the central office leader in charge of teaching and learning is principal development. Learning about and implementing school improvement processes must be a central theme for principal professional development throughout the year. Schools in a system will be at varying stages of performance. If all schools are going to thrive in a system, this diversity must be used to drive higher levels of performance throughout the system. It is the responsibility of the central office administrator to transform the system; this transformation

Table 5.4 Reflective Questions for Monitoring Development of the
School Improvement Plan

Questions	Evidence
How involved are the faculty members in developing the plan?	
Do goals match the school's data?	
Do the goals support the district vision for improving instruction?	
Do the strategies reasonably accomplish the goal?	
If the school fully implements this strategy, would the objective be accomplished?	
Do the action steps support the strategies?	
Are they reasonable in both scope and sequence?	
Does the proposed timeline seem reasonable?	
Could a school reasonably accomplish the action steps in the coming year?	
Can those action steps be accomplished sufficiently in that timeframe?	
How will the school know the goal is accomplished? The strategies? The action steps?	
Can this plan be used for professional development efforts?	
Is this an authentic working plan or a document to fulfill requirements for the district?	
Can leaders use this plan for differentiated supervision to help teachers improve instruction?	
Does this plan offer a hope for improved academic achievement for this school?	

depends on excellent practice being developed, shared, demonstrated, and adopted across and between schools (Hopkins, 2008). Lateral capacity is developed when principals have an opportunity to share plans, successes, and missteps with colleagues.

Central office administrators need to organize professional development so that small groups of principals implementing the same strategies can learn from each other *throughout* the year. Thus, the central office administrator needs to implement a long-range plan for professional development for principals that focuses on enhancing both content (pedagogy) and process (school improvement) knowledge (see Chapter 8 for more specifics). During the fall it is critical for central office to make sure principals have the support they need to implement/revise plans; providing opportunities for deep learning is vital.

 ## Move 3: Give Feedback

Constructive feedback on an ongoing basis is a necessity for improvement (Fullan, 2014). Developing and implementing a school improvement plan is a developmental process and this process can be accelerated when leaders are provided meaningful feedback, information that aims to reduce the gap between what is now and what should or could be (Hattie & Timperley, 2007). Feedback is most powerful when used in a learning context; thus it is critical that during the fall principals receive feedback from their central office administrator regarding their plan.

When reviewing plans, the central office leader needs to consider whether the goals and strategies align to the district's strategic plan and initiatives. This doesn't mean that each school will have the same cookie-cutter plan with the exact same goals and strategies, but it does mean that schools in the system need to position themselves so that when their plans are fully implemented it impacts district goals through complementing district initiatives. Marzano and Waters' (2009) concept of "defined autonomy," where an organization establishes and maintains clear operating procedures while *simultaneously* supporting constrained improvisation, is the goal here. For example, if a district has adopted the gradual release of responsibility as the instructional framework (Fisher & Frey, 2014), then some buildings may focus on collaborative group work as a strategy and others may concentrate on focus lessons. The focus for the school improvement plan will be based on their data and observations.

Central office staff need to set a clear deadline for plan submission. The authors typically had a deadline of late August, allowing principals to review the plan with existing staff and engage new staff. Within two weeks of submission, written feedback was given to the building principal. Written feedback was designed to help principals develop a focused plan. Proficiency statements for each part of the plan were included in order to reinforce understanding and to help principals align goals, strategies, action steps, and professional development. Appendix D includes an example of the feedback form.

Have to Do: Develop Look Fors

Schools that have plans that include monitoring, evaluation, and inquiry experience significantly greater gains in student achievement than schools who omit these elements (Reeves, 2009). A critical component in the monitoring and evaluation process is the development of look fors. A look for is a clear statement that describes an *observable* teaching or learning behavior, strategy, outcome, product, or procedure (Mooney & Mausbach, 2008). Identifying what the strategies look like and sound like when implemented is the first step in effective monitoring. The use of collaboratively developed look fors unifies a school by helping create shared meaning and a common focus. Look fors help establish standards for what the innovations in the plan will look like when fully implemented. When used consistently throughout the school, look fors help bridge the gap between learning and implementation.

Development of Look Fors

On the surface, the development of look fors is a conceptually simple, straightforward practice. However, there are complexities to the process and use that if ignored will render the look fors irrelevant. The keys to developing look fors are as follows:

1. *All staff must collaboratively develop look fors.* The purpose of having a set of look fors is to help staff understand what the strategies in the plan will look like when they are in place. In a heightened sense of urgency to get the look fors developed, a leader may be tempted to develop a list and hand them out or, worse, use some developed by another school. It is both the process and the product that matter. Developing look fors as a faculty helps the staff develop shared meaning, clarify misconceptions, and deepen ownership of the plan.

2. *Look fors must be directly connected to the school improvement plan.* One of the primary purposes of look fors is to operationalize the school improvement plan. Thus, look fors must describe the strategies in the plan. Effective school improvement plans provide focus for a school and aligned look fors are essential for intense focus.

3. *Look fors can't be developed in the absence of knowledge, but understand it is a developmental process.* One of the biggest benefits of developing look fors is that the process deepens teachers' understanding of the initiative being implemented. This happens by engaging staff in learning around the initiative before developing the list. Without providing time for learning, the look fors may not be detailed or useful enough to provide feedback. The saying "you don't know what you don't know" is apropos here. Deep meaning will occur as they implement; learning is the work (Fullan, 2009). Table 5.5 is an example of two sets of look fors developed on the same topic by relatively the same staff over the course of a year. It is evident from this example how the staff's understanding developed over the course of the year. Look fors are a vehicle for learning. Understanding will develop through implementation.

4. *Look fors must be observable.* They must be something that can be seen or heard. Look fors provide evidence of strategy implementation. They help a leader focus observations so meaningful feedback can be provided. Consider the difference between the two look fors in Table 5.6.

Look For A leaves too much up to interpretation for both the teacher and the principal, while Look For B provides a more specific expectation. A principal can talk to students in the classroom and gather information about what students can and can't do. The key is to make sure that the look fors are observable.

Table 5.5 Look For Comparisons

The following look fors were developed for math intervention practices provided by classroom teachers (Tier 1). The emboldened sections indicate the changes made after the team implemented and furthered their study on this topic.

January 27

- Teacher is working with a small group of students or one on one.
- Teacher works with a small group of students.
- Students practice a specific skill.
- Other students are working on a game or part of their investigation.
- Teacher has a clear focus for the intervention time.
- Teacher is prompting students with questions and using talk moves.
- Teacher is using precise mathematical language and holding students accountable to use it as well.

March 24

- **Teacher scaffolds from concrete to semi-concrete to abstract representations.**
- **Small group of students are listening and watching teacher's explicit instruction.**
- **Content is connected to life skills.**
- **Teacher think-aloud begins at student level (based on previous data).**
- **Teacher shows examples and counterexamples.**
- **Teacher frequently stops the group to clarify and directly highlight critical concepts and understanding.**
- Other students are working on a game or part of their investigation.
- Teacher has a clear focus for the intervention time.
- Teacher is prompting students with questions and using talk moves.
- Teacher is using precise mathematical language and holding students accountable to use it as well.
  - o **Teacher is using terminology that is easily understood by students.**
  - o **Vocabulary is recorded/referenced/reviewed/reinforced throughout the lesson.**
- **Teacher follows the model-prompt-practice sequence.**
- **Students are given similar examples for independent practice at the completion of the lesson.**

(Used with permission from Garry Milbourn, Longfellow Elementary)

Table 5.6 Example Look Fors

Look For A:
Evidence of rigor and relevance.
Look For B:
Students know the purpose for learning and can articulate thinking strategies.

Reflective Questions

Development Stage

- Is the *look for* more than one or two words?
- Is the *look for* a complete thought or sentence?
- Is the *look for* something you could **see or hear** if you walked into a classroom?
- Is the *look for* written in plain language that a non-educator could understand?

Refinement Stage

- Do the staff need to do more learning in order to revise look fors?
- Did the look fors help to provide clarity and meaningful feedback?
- Are there look fors that are no longer needed because all staff have institutionalized a practice?

Principal Moves

Move 1: Collaboratively Define Look Fors

All staff need to be included in development of look fors. Typically this can occur over the course of two 90-minute meetings. During the first meeting staff members are asked to individually write five to seven statements that answer the question, "What would this strategy (i.e., formative assessment, higher order thinking, productive groupwork . . .) look like and sound like in our classrooms and school?" Once individual lists are developed, staff move into small groups and share lists, identifying common look fors and categorizing into three different areas: teacher behaviors, student behaviors, and environment. Each look for from the consolidated lists from the team is written on a Post-it note. Post-it notes are gathered and posted under the corresponding category: teacher behaviors, student behaviors, and environment. Staff are divided into three teams (or six depending on the size of the faculty) and asked to review one of the three categories, narrowing the list so that each category has five to seven look fors. After these are developed, staff carousel around the room reviewing lists, posting questions or comments. These lists are gathered and reviewed by the leadership team for editing prior to the second meeting. During the second meeting the edited lists are shared, staff review in small groups, and questions are answered to help ensure clarity and clear up misconceptions. At the end of this meeting you have the school's official look for list.

It is easy to get caught up in wordsmithing and belaboring this process until the look fors are "just right." The look fors are an indicator of the learning of staff at that moment in time; they will improve as the staff continue to learn and implement. There is no such thing as a perfect look for list; it is impossible to attain. Don't let this impede implementation efforts. The look fors developed in Table 5.5 in March are an improvement on the look fors developed in January; however, the January list still helps teachers improve their practice. Look fors will improve over time; the key is to begin to identify the look fors and use them.

Move 2: Provide Feedback Using Look Fors

Principals need to use the collaboratively developed look fors to provide feedback after walkthroughs. Walkthroughs are the vehicle to determine if the school improvement plan is being implemented, and at what levels, and to identify what support staff need next in order to get to deeper levels of implementation. The four fundamentals of the walkthrough process are focusing, walking, reflecting, and feedback. Look fors provide the focus and that is why it is critical that they are developed with all staff and are clearly stated. Feedback to staff is based on the look fors. Using collaboratively developed look fors around strategies identified in the school improvement plan ensures that the walkthrough isn't an inspection or

Table 5.7 Feedback Methods

	RATIONALE	TIP
Validate Practice	Raises level of awareness and promotes likelihood will occur again	Be specific & include why this is important

Example:
For example, one set of students was being asked to respond in writing to a series of important quotes from the novel they were reading. They had to describe the significance of the quote and what it implied about the character—very high-level activities. By using writing as a thinking strategy this teacher can get a clear sense of EACH student's level of connection with the text without using knowledge or comprehension-level questions.

Notice Approximations	Pushes the goals of school plan and professional development	Compliment and encourage

Example:
When your students work in groups the level of engagement increases. Keep experimenting with ways to ease the transitions between whole group and small group activities. You and your students are making great progress. Bravo!

Foster Reflection	Causes staff to reflect about their own practice, nudges teachers in the direction you want them to go	Start with phrases like "I am wondering . . ." "I would be interested to know . . ."

Example:
How do we help our students answer the question "What am I expected to learn by studying this unit?" Also, we need to consider, as we begin each new unit, the positive impact of using pre-assessment strategies such as anticipation/reaction guides to determine what prior knowledge the students have. We will begin to wrestle with these questions as we develop our SIP and PD plans for next year.

"gotcha." The staff know what the principal is looking for and know that feedback will validate the teaching and learning practices found in the "look fors."

The leader's commitment to a growth mindset is manifested in the type of feedback given after walkthroughs. The purpose of feedback is to help staff grow or "lift" staff. This doesn't happen by pointing out deficits; rather growth occurs when practices that are aligned with look fors are validated. Three primary methods for feedback are used that align with a growth mindset: validating good practice, noticing close approximations, and encouraging reflection (Mooney & Mausbach, 2008). Table 5.7 provides an overview of each of these methods.

Look fors are effective when they are used. This means that a principal needs to give feedback on these at a minimum once a week. The rule of thumb for the authors has been to visit every classroom at least once a week using look fors and providing feedback. In larger schools this means dividing classrooms or content areas between other building level administrators. If the look fors are clear, a building administrative team will be able to give focused feedback. The key is to provide feedback. Feedback can be one-on-one, in a small group, or to the entire faculty, and can be either written or face-to-face. The level of implementation and the amount of time staff have been implementing a strategy will determine which method is most effective. The critical point is to *give feedback* after every walk-through.

Central Office Move

Move: Provide Feedback on Look Fors and Accompanying Feedback

Using look fors and providing feedback to staff around the look fors is a developmental process. In order to support principals as they learn to use this powerful tool, the central office administrator needs to review look fors and feedback letters. This practice helps not only with accountability, but also ensures that these tools are used properly so they can have maximum impact. All too frequently effective processes get diluted or dropped because the leader didn't realize the desired effect. The issue many times isn't the tool, but the use of the tool. Giving feedback on look fors and feedback to staff helps to ensure quality, deepens principals' under-standing, and addresses misconceptions. Ann remembers a time when she reviewed a feedback letter to staff that was extremely negative pointing out to staff all of the things they weren't doing well. If left unchecked and the principal continued to provide feedback in this vein, a serious culture problem would have developed. By reviewing the feedback Ann was able to work directly with this principal, helping him understand how to use these letters to validate and teach staff. Ann typically reviewed the look fors and feedback letters once a year for all principals, but would differentiate on the frequency depending on the experience of the administrator or their level of implementation with the tools.

Have to Do: Differentiate Supervision for Staff

The idea of differentiating instruction to accommodate the different ways that students learn is an approach to teaching that advocates active planning for student differences in classrooms (Tomlinson & Allan, 2000). This same approach needs to be in place when supervising teachers. Differentiated supervision of personnel means that school leaders need to do things differently based on what individual teachers need and what students deserve (Mooney & Mausbach, 2008). Differentiated supervision embraces a philosophy that is designed to match the level of supervision with the needs and competencies of individuals. Leaders need to be able to differentiate based on both teacher needs and supervision practices.

Differentiation by Teacher. Differentiating supervision by teacher means knowing and understanding the needs of individual teachers. Whitaker (2002) has identified and aptly named three different types of teachers: superstars, backbones, and mediocres. While these may be broad categories with not all teachers sharing the exact same characteristics, understanding the distinctions is useful in helping a leader adjust supervision practices. For example, a leader's inclination may be to get out of the way of the superstars, leaving them alone to "do their thing." However, superstars are continually striving to improve their practice, thus "leaving them alone" may cause resentment or frustration. A leader with a growth mindset knows that superstars are often the early implementers for new initiatives; providing support to them via feedback not only helps ensure that new strategies will be implemented with fidelity, but promotes large-scale implementation due to the respect they garner from the majority of the faculty.

All teachers need feedback to improve; however, the type of feedback will vary based on the teacher type. Hattie and Timperley (2007) identified different levels of feedback. These levels can help an administrator begin to discern which type will be most effective with the three different types of teachers. The first level is concerned with the task or the product. This level of feedback is information-focused and leads to acquiring more or different information. This type of feedback has been called corrective feedback and is the type that may be used most frequently with new and mediocre teachers. New and mediocre teachers haven't yet acquired the skills they need to be effective, so explicit and direct feedback is necessary. Level one feedback to teachers may sound like, "When sharing 'today's goal' you turned your back and changed your thinking and created a talk bubble and then sort of worked the criteria out, out loud. This was very confusing to your students. In the future you need to make sure that you are clear on the goal for the day and state that explicitly. Let's work on developing one together."

The next level of feedback is aimed at the processing of information or learning processes used to complete a task. This type of feedback helps reduce cognitive load, provide strategies for detecting errors, rethink approaches to the tasks, cue to seek more effective information, and employ task strategies. This feedback will be used frequently with both mediocre and backbone teachers. For example, a principal may say, "Students' comparing and contrasting examples were very basic. What do you think was the reason? Let's revisit depth of knowledge (DOK) for your questions." Process feedback is more effective than task feedback at deepening understanding.

The third level of feedback is focused on students monitoring their learning or developing self-regulation. This type of feedback helps self-evaluate skills, promotes task persistence, increases acceptance and asking for feedback, and increases effort into seeking and using feedback information. This type of feedback will most frequently be used with backbones and superstars. For example, "Students were able to articulate their purpose for reading and what they were practicing. How did you accomplish this?" Feedback about the process or self-regulation is especially powerful as it helps teachers become consciously competent.

The distinctions between these three levels of feedback are important because not all feedback is created equal, or in other words will not end up having the desired effect, especially if the type of teacher (new, mediocre, backbone, superstar) receiving the feedback isn't considered. The feedback levels aren't mutually exclusive to teacher types. For example, a mediocre teacher shouldn't always just receive task feedback. Feedback about task is effective when used in combination with process and self-regulation information. Differentiated supervision requires the leader to understand what level of feedback will be most effective in addressing individual teacher needs. Knowing where teachers are functioning helps the leader make these decisions.

Differentiation by Practice. Differentiation by practice means using a variety of supervision methods to provide support to teachers. These practices include, but are not limited to, general walkthroughs, focused walkthroughs, implementation studies, peer observations, coaching cycles, professional learning communities, and formal evaluations. All of these methods are necessary to provide the leader with an in-depth understanding of the needs of the teacher. Effective leaders understand that observing teachers two to three times a year and creating a summative report will not help teachers improve practice or impact student results. The leader's commitment to a growth mindset requires that teachers have multiple opportunities to learn and grow, and a leader needs to use multiple methods to make this happen.

Reflective Questions

Development Stage

- Where are staff in terms of superstar, backbone, and mediocre categories?
- What impact do these distinctions have on type of feedback needed?
- Is the infrastructure in place to support differentiated supervision practices?

Refinement Stage

- Which staff members have moved in terms of superstar, backbone, and mediocre?
- Which supervision practices need refinement?
- Do any adjustments need to be made to schedules in order to ensure that supervision practices are conducted on an ongoing basis?

Principal Moves

Move 1: Align Individual Professional Growth Plans to School Improvement Plan

While the methodologies for providing support to teachers are varied, this doesn't mean that the focus for supervision should be. The school improvement plan provides focus, and supervision practices need to be in alignment with the plan. Individual professional growth plans required by many districts' formal evaluation process should align to school goals and professional development efforts. Teachers should have sufficient opportunities to learn and practice an innovation before they are observed. Using strategies from the school improvement plan as a focus for individual growth ensures that the teacher will be provided these opportunities. A climate of trust and respect is cultivated when individual professional growth plans are aligned with the school improvement plan since the goals and strategies are developed collaboratively. Teachers have a clear picture of what is expected via look fors, eliminating the "gotcha" feeling that is often associated with supervision efforts.

Move 2: Monitor Feedback Efforts

Differentiated supervision requires leaders to develop a method for tracking feedback to staff. Tracking feedback is critical because it helps the leader monitor growth of a teacher over time and it guarantees individualization. Whether providing written feedback via Post-it notes or face-to-face feedback, this information needs to be captured as much as possible. This data is just as valuable as teachers' anecdotal records on students and as such needs to be used to help plan professional learning, communicate with the teacher, and track progress over time. Tools such as Voxer or voice recording using a smartphone, with the data importing into a Google spreadsheet, are easy and simple methods that don't require an inordinate amount of principal time. The key is to identify a method for capturing the data and then using this data throughout the year to help provide support.

Central Office Move

 Move: Provide Coaching Visits to Principals

Coaching visits are one-on-one meetings with the principal and a central office administrator. The purpose of these visits is to support the principal on issues in their building.

These "power hours" typically consist of 30 minutes of reviewing implementation efforts that may include conversations with students, analyzing work displays, or walking through classrooms. The second half-hour focuses on items the principal wants to discuss. A minimum expectation is to conduct these visits monthly; however, some schools may receive more support based on their data and the tenure of the principal. Depending on the size of the organization, these visits are typically done at the director level. Information shared during these meetings helps central office staff stay connected to the real work in schools. This approach, while time-consuming, helps create a symbiotic system, where everyone learns from one another rather than a top-down system. Lessons learned from time in schools with principals help to shape the focus and direction of initiatives and professional learning, rather than having central office make these decisions in isolation or out of context of the real work.

Summary

Engaging staff in the school improvement plan, developing look fors, and differentiating supervision for staff must be addressed in the fall. The use of these critical processes and the accompanying moves helps leaders live by the commitments, resulting in an effective and efficient system for teaching and learning.

Planting a Seed: Using the Right Tools

Ann was attempting to hang a picture in her office and is completely challenged when it comes to anything handy. Hanging a picture definitely falls in this category for her. The wall where she wanted to hang the picture was cement, but lucky for her there was already a screw/nail in the exact location where she wanted to place her picture. The problem was the nail/screw was inserted too far into the wall; it just needed to come out of the wall a little bit so the picture would be able to be safely displayed. With great confidence and gusto she used a small hammer and tried to pry the screw out of the wall ever so slightly. For those of you with the handy gene, you know what happened next. Plaster dust came spewing out everywhere, bits of plaster and dust went all over, and she now had a big hole where the nail/screw used to be. Talk about making more work . . . she now needed to putty the hole, repaint the hole, drill a new hole, and clean up the dust and plaster. How different this scenario would have been if she had used the right tool in the first place (which, for the record, is a screwdriver).

Does this same thing ever happen to us in our school improvement efforts? How many times do we cause ourselves more work or slow down progress by not using the most effective tool? Consider some of the following common school improvement *construction* issues and consider some of the tools that might help you get out of a jam.

- *Construction Issue*: Staff have not bought into improvement initiatives or are unaware of efforts.

- *Tool (SIP)*: Go back and rework your school improvement plan so that it is targeted and focused. Heed Fullan's (2009) advice and make sure it is a skinny plan that has focused outcomes. Make sure all staff have ownership in development, including what data will be collected along the way to monitor progress.

- *Construction Issue*: Staff are not implementing what is being learned during professional development.

- *Tools (look fors and walkthroughs)*: Make sure that you have developed look fors with your staff about what it looks like and sounds like when the strategy is implemented. Then use these look fors on your walk-throughs and provide specific feedback to both individuals and the entire staff. Remember that your feedback needs to validate the practices you find that match your look fors.

- *Construction Issue*: Staff are resistant to trying new things, reluctant to change.

- *Tool (data)*: Use student data from both state and district assessments to help staff identify strengths and areas for growth. Conduct data analysis during PLC time so all staff have the opportunity to look at data regarding their students.

- *Construction Issue*: Staff are implementing strategies outlined in the SIP out of compliance, rather than understanding benefits for students.

- *Tool (PD plan)*: Revisit your PD plan and either slow down or take a couple steps back and consider what structures need to be in place to get staff to deeper levels of understanding.

In each of these incidents you can use a different tool, but think about the consequences when we use the wrong ones (i.e., confusion, discontent, lack of improved achievement). Ann's picture has been hung, but is a little crooked and there is still some visible evidence of the damage she has done. Next time she will step back before she jumps in and make sure she uses the right tool. It will save a lot of damage in the long run.

References

Dufour, R., Dufour, R., Eaker, R., & Many, T. (2012). *Learning by doing: A handbook for professional learning communities at work.* Bloomington, IN: Solution Tree Press.

Fisher, D., & Frey, N. (2014). *Better teaching through structured learning: A framework for the gradual release of responsibility,* 2nd ed. Alexandria, VA: ASCD.

Fullan, M. (2009). *Motion leadership: The skinny on becoming change savvy.* Thousand Oaks, CA: Corwin Press.

Fullan, M. (2014). *The principal: Three keys to maximizing impact.* San Francisco, CA: Jossey-Bass.

Hargreaves, A., & Fullan, M. (2012). *Professional capital: Transforming teaching in every school.* New York: Teachers College Press & Toronto: Ontario Principals Council.

Hattie, J., & Timperley, H. (2007). The power of feedback. *Review of Educational Research, 77* (1), 81–112.

Hopkins, D. (2008). Realising the potential of system leadership. In Pont, B., Nusche, D., & Hopkins, D. (Eds.), *Improving school leadership, volume 2: Case studies on system leadership* (pages 13–35), 2nd ed. Paris: Organisation for Economic Co-operation and Development.

Kluger, J. (2009). *Simplexity: Why simple things become complex (and how complex things can become simple).* New York: Hyperion Books.

Marzano, R. J., Pickering, D., & Pollock, J. E. (2001). *Classroom instruction that works: Research-based strategies for increasing student achievement.* Alexandria, VA: ASCD.

Marzano, R. J., & Waters, T. (2009). *District leadership that works: Striking the right balance.* Bloomington, IN: Solution Tree.

Mooney, N., & Mausbach, A. (2008). *Align the design: A blueprint for school improvement.* Alexandria, VA: ASCD.

Robinson, V. M. J. (2014). *Student-centered leadership.* Hoboken, NJ: Jossey-Bass.

Senge, P. (2011). *Schools that learn: A fifth discipline fieldbook for educators, parents, and everyone who cares about education.* New York: Nicholas Brealey.

Stiggins, R. (2014). *Revolutionize assessment: Empower students, inspire learning.* Thousand Oakes, CA: Corwin Press.

Tomlinson, C. A., & Allan, S. D. (2000). *Leadership for differentiating schools and classrooms.* Alexandria, VA: ASCD.

Whitaker, T. (2002). *Dealing with difficult teachers.* New York, NY: Eye on Education.

Winter

Making the Work Happen through Implementation and Monitoring

A garden is a grand teacher. It teaches patience and careful watchfulness; it teaches industry and thrift; above all it teaches entire trust.

Gertrude Jekyll

Planting a garden is strenuous work. Once the garden is planted, however, the real labor begins, and while this work may not be as physically demanding, it does require a great deal of attentiveness. Not only does the gardener need to water and fertilize on a regular basis, they also need to trust the growing process, allowing plants the time they need to grow, while making sure the conditions are right—removing the weeds or bugs that may impede growth. Successful gardeners understand not all plants in their garden will require the same amount of sun or water, and they adjust their care accordingly.

During the winter season, school leaders must use the same precise consideration, keeping a careful eye on the school improvement plan, letting it take root while also responding to the diverse needs of the students and staff in the school. The "have to dos" in the winter include:

- Have to Do: Monitor the plan.
- Have to Do: Develop teachers by responding to individual student needs.
- Have to Do: Embed the mission in the work.

Have to Do: Monitor the Plan

There are three general methods principals use when monitoring school improvement efforts. These include general walkthroughs, focused walkthroughs, and implementation studies. Each of these methods is an effective and necessary tool that helps the school leader track implementation efforts and the impact on teaching and learning. Table 6.1 provides an overview of all three methods. While the methods differ in purpose, the common critical feature is the use of feedback.

General Walkthrough

The general walkthrough is defined as an organized visit through the school's learning areas to observe teaching and learning. The general walkthrough advocated by these authors has four fundamental steps that distinguish this process from other methods. The fundamentals of general walkthroughs include focusing, walking, reflection, and feedback. Table 6.2 outlines the general walkthrough process.

Focus. Before a leader sets foot in a classroom to conduct a general walkthrough they must define what they are looking for in a way that doesn't leave any unanswered questions. Collaboratively developed look fors aligned to the school improvement plan (see Chapter 5) must be in place. The use of look fors assists teachers and administrators in focusing on specific aspects of teaching and learning. Look fors narrow the focus to achievable and identifiable improvements and build unity of purpose.

Walk. Once the look fors are firmly in place the leader needs to walk through the school, letting staff know the focus for the walkthrough. A critical practice for the general walkthrough is to review samples of student work posted in hallways and in work folders and to talk to students. The purpose of the general walkthrough is to ensure that the strategies in the plan are being implemented at high levels, resulting in changes in student achievement. The general walkthrough is not an announced visit so it is difficult to hit every classroom at that exact moment when the teacher is engaged in using identified strategies; thus it is imperative to take time to talk to students and examine work. Examining student work and talking to students is the

Table 6.1 Monitoring Methods

	General Walkthrough	Focused Walkthrough	Implementation Study
Description	Organized visit through a school's learning areas, using specific look fors to focus on teaching and learning Observation 3–5 minutes per class	Observe teaching and learning in a specific grade level or content area Observation 10–20 minutes in length	Scheduled visits to measure quantitative data on SIP implementation Time varies depending on the strategy
Purpose	Identify building-wide trends and patterns regarding implementation of SIP in order to help determine "next steps" for PD	Learn instructional strengths and needs of individual teachers Follow up on learning from PLC	Determine how near or far the school is from reaching 100 percent implementation of strategies in SIP
Frequency	Daily	Depends on work in small group PD, but on average each teacher every two weeks	Approximately two to three times per year
Feedback Method	Face-to-face school-wide	Face-to-face email/note	School-wide face-to-face

Table 6.2 General Walkthrough Fundamentals

FOCUS	• Develop look fors • Communicate look fors
WALK	• Talk to students • 3–5 minutes in each learning environment, focus on look fors • Review samples of student work posted in hallways, in work folders
REFLECT	• What did you see? • What does it mean?
GIVE FEEDBACK	• Validate, Validate, Validate

only way to determine if the strategies being implemented are working. Artifacts such as student notebooks, work displays, and anchor charts should also be examined. Looking at the outputs (student learning) rather than inputs (teacher behavior) makes this a student-centered process and is more palatable to teachers. Common questions to ask students when in classrooms include:

● What did you do by learning this assignment that you didn't know before?

● What does your teacher want you to learn by doing this lesson?

● What have you learned this year that is helping you be a better reader or writer?

● How does this lesson connect to what you learned yesterday?

● How do you know when you have done quality work?

Reflect. Once the walkthrough is complete, the principal needs to take time to reflect on what was seen. A busy principal rarely has time to reflect immediately after completing a general walkthough, so it is recommended to have some method of collecting information from the visit. It is easy to voice-record on a smartphone what was observed, or use the tried and true notepaper on a clipboard. The key is to document enough information so that rich reflection can occur. During reflection the principal needs to be able to identify what was observed that "hit the mark" (matched the look fors), determine how many classrooms demonstrated the look fors, and identify next steps by looking at trends and patterns across classrooms.

Give Feedback. Feedback is required after every general walkthrough. Feedback methods were outlined in Figure 5.7. The key to feedback is to validate and teach. Using examples of teaching and learning taken from the classrooms in their school provides concrete examples for teachers and helps them see that strategies can be successful in their context. The authors have found that it is important to provide whole staff, small group, and individual feedback. The stage the staff are at in implementing the SIP determines which type of feedback may be used with more frequency. For example, if a building is in the first year of implementation and the staff are being asked to implement a brand new strategy, more whole staff feedback may be needed so that all staff can learn what implementation looks like in practice. Leaders need to identify the methods and techniques that work best for them. A combination of whole staff, small group (via PLCs), and individual feedback ensures that feedback will be given. The key is to make sure that feedback is given after *each* walkthrough and that it validates or notices close approximations and causes reflection. Appendix E provides an example of feedback from a general walkthrough.

Focused Walkthrough

The focused walkthrough is designed to target observations of teaching and learning for a longer period of time (10–20 minutes) in a classroom or series of classrooms. The focused walkthrough is used when the leader wants to follow up or learn more around a teaching and learning issue that has arisen either through the general walkthrough or PLC meetings. Like Marshall's (2013) mini observations, the focused walkthrough allows the leader to home in on specific instructional issues in order to help either (a) diagnose why results aren't happening for students, or (b) reinforce/refine teachers' implementation of a new strategy. The look fors in a focused walkthrough are identified when working with a teacher or small groups of teachers, so they are clearly aware of the purpose of the walkthrough, and it may or may not be scheduled in advance. For example, specificity of language during student conferences would be an area of study for a focused walkthrough. Like general walkthroughs the key is to make sure that teachers have a clear understanding of the focus of the observations. Feedback is a critical component and typically face-to-face feedback is both the easiest and the most powerful since teachers have been working on the issue and are anxious to have a discussion around what was observed. Appendix E provides an example of feedback from a focused walkthrough.

Implementation Study

An implementation study is a scheduled visit to measure quantitative data on school improvement plan implementation. The goal with the school improvement plan is 100 percent implementation or, in the words of Nancy Mooney, "The work isn't done until every child benefits from the innovation." An implementation study is designed to help the leader determine how near or far the school is from 100 percent implementation. Implementation studies are conducted two to three times a year and the data is used to help the principal refine practice and determine next steps. For example, if the strategy in the school improvement plan is to implement focus lessons based on Fisher and Frey's (2013) work on gradual release, the principal would schedule visits to every classroom throughout the school during a focus lesson. Depending on the size of the school and the number of assistant principals, this could take two to three weeks to complete. Again, the look fors developed around focus lessons would be used. Data collected would be analyzed around which look fors are in place and which need additional work. This analysis helps the principal and the leadership team identify what additional supports in the form of professional development are needed. An example of implementation study data and feedback is found in Appendix E.

Reflective Questions

Development Stage

- Are look fors being used to provide feedback?
- Is the evidence of strategy implementation data being collected helpful in determining next steps?
- Am I conducting walkthroughs (focused and general) on a weekly basis?

Refinement Stage

● What can be learned about the school from the strategy implementation data?

● If more than one implementation study was conducted during the year, how did the data change over the course of the year?

● Was the right data collected in order to discern levels of implementation and next steps?

● Do look fors need to be revisited? Is additional learning needed to deepen understanding?

● Am I providing feedback consistently?

Principal Moves

Move 1: Conduct Walkthroughs

The quality of leadership is second only to teachers in regard to impact on student achievement (Louis, Leithwood, Wahlstrom, & Anderson, 2010; Robinson, Lloyd, & Rowe, 2008). Successful leaders spend a significant portion of time leading teaching and learning and this can't be done from an office. Walkthroughs are part of the action research process in the school that provides data. Stringer (2007) defines this as "look, think, act, and look again." The purpose of a school is to promote learning. Even though other management issues may require attention from the school leader, principals must proactively plan for walkthroughs. Principals must make general and focused walkthroughs a priority by ensuring they become a daily part of their routine.

The most obvious method of organization is intentionally planning on a calendar each week. Typically, a principal should schedule 30 minutes a day for general walkthroughs and 30 minutes a day for focused walkthroughs. These walkthroughs provide ongoing qualitative data about the school; the implementation study that is conducted two to three times a year also provides qualitative data. Principals must make it a priority to work with teachers and students during school hours. Scheduling office hours and utilizing the time before and after school to work with teachers helps accomplish this. Table 6.3 provides an example of a sample schedule for a building principal.

Table 6.3 Sample Schedules

	Sample Schedule (Walkthrough Focus): Secondary
7–7:45 am	Office hours: managerial duties: email, telephone calls, planning day
7:45–8 am	Relationship building with students and staff greeting as students arrive
8–8:30 am	Classroom visits: relationship building with students, monitoring behaviors
8:30–9 am	PLC (teacher development content specific)
9–9:30 am	Focused walkthrough specific focus on content
9:30–10 am	Planning for professional development including PLC
10–10:30 am	PLC (teacher development content specific)
10:30–11 am	Focused walkthrough specific focus on content
11–11:30 am	Office hours (managerial duties: email, telephone calls)
11:30 am–12 pm	General walkthrough (feedback on look fors)
12–1 pm	Working lunch planning with teacher leaders/assistants
1–1:30 pm	PLC (teacher development content specific)
1:30–2 pm	Focused walkthrough specific focus on content
2–3 pm	Office/building hours for student and teacher needs
3–5:30 pm	Office hours: meeting with teachers, central office, curriculum planning . . .

Note: Teacher observations and instructional planning can be substituted during these times as necessary.

Sample Schedule (Walkthrough Focus): Elementary

7:30–8:15 am	Office hours: managerial duties: email, telephone calls, planning day
8:15 –9 am	Grade level PLC; students arrive at 8:45, class covered by support staff
9–9:30 am	Classroom visits: relationship building with students, monitoring behaviors
9:30–10 am	General or focused walkthrough
10–10:30 am	Office hours: managerial duties: email, telephone calls
10:30–11:15 am	Grade level PLC
11:15–11:30 am	Relationship building with students and staff (i.e., lunch room)
11:30 am–12 pm	General or focused walkthrough (feedback on look fors)
12–1 pm	Working lunch planning with teacher leaders
1–1:30 pm	Planning for professional development including PLC
1:30–2 pm	Focused walkthrough specific focus on content
2–3 pm	Office/building hours for student and teacher needs
3:30–4:15 pm	Grade level PLC
4:15–6 pm	Office hours: meeting with teachers, central office, curriculum planning . . .

Note: Teacher observations and instructional planning can be substituted during these times as necessary.

When conducting walkthroughs a principal needs to identify the tools that will help them deliver feedback in the most efficient manner. Kim's toolkit includes her laptop, the school's radio, a pen/pencil, Post-its, the look fors, and a clipboard. When she was getting started with the process she also included a list of questions she wanted to ask students. Kim uses these tools because she provides immediate feedback on a Post-it after she leaves each room. Other principals use all-electronic methods to provide feedback. The key is to identify the tools you need and make sure that you have them as you conduct walkthroughs.

Move 2: Use Displays of Student Work to Reinforce Learning

Student work displays provide a window into the classroom. Displays help parents, teachers, administrators, and students understand the learning that is occurring in the school. For parents this means getting a deeper understanding of the content the students are learning and what quality looks like. For teachers displays provide models of effective tasks and assessments and can help them see the articulation of the curriculum throughout the school. For principals it gives a glimpse of the depth of student understanding and provides another vehicle to monitor school improvement efforts. It is impossible when conducting general walkthroughs to catch every teacher at just that right moment when they are implementing SIP strategies, which is why student displays are so important. Examining student work provides the principal with in-depth insights on both the teaching and learning in the classroom.

In addition to helping the principal monitor the school improvement plan, displays of student work communicate very clearly what is valued in the school. According to Ted Sizer (2004), excellent schools include strong models of what good work should be so that the whole school community can see. Lower-performing schools' work displays are either non-existent or decorated with commercially prepared posters that only superficially relate to the curriculum and have limited connections to student learning. What is being communicated if the walls in classrooms and hallways are blank? If the walls in a school include displays of student work that post student papers all in a row with fill-in-the-blank responses, what is the message? Is it that learning is a process, or that the answer is most important? How does the school communicate that learning is valued?

Here are some general guidelines regarding displays of student work:

- *Make it purposeful.* One of the objectives of displaying work is to extend learning. Displays that don't include the purpose of the learning make it more difficult for students (and other visitors) to understand why this content was important. Teachers need to post work that not only demonstrates learning aligned to standards but also the process for getting there. Just posting student papers isn't enough; the what and why are critical so connections to learning can be made by students and the adults in the school. Including feedback from the teacher or peers is one way to make this connection.

- *Highlight the process of learning.* Learning is complex work and students need to understand that it is as much about how they arrive at a learning target as it is about the arrival or "answer." Displays should show a progression of understanding that showcases the process for learning rich content.

- *Keep it current.* If the walls are an extension of our learning then having something displayed in December that was learned in September doesn't help students see the relevance in their current learning and doesn't help the principal monitor recent teaching and learning.

- *Include students in the design.* That the person doing the most work is the one doing the learning holds true for student displays. Students should be allowed to articulate what they learned and why and this should be included in the display.

Central Office Moves

Move 1: Conduct Supervisory Walkthroughs Looking for Schools Look Fors

A supervisory walkthrough is an opportunity for the principal and the central office administrator(s) in charge of teaching and learning to walk through the school together to monitor school improvement efforts. The supervisory walkthrough allows the central office administrator to provide mentoring and support to the building principal. It raises the bar of accountability for implementing school improvement initiatives. This process provides concrete help for principals regarding leading teaching and learning at their school and helps develop and maintain a relationship of trust and respect between the central office administrator and the principal.

The process for the supervisory walkthrough is similar to the principal building walkthroughs. The steps include planning and pre-briefing, walking, debriefing, and following up with feedback. The planning stage includes scheduling the walkthrough. Typically the central office administrator will designate several dates on their calendar and allow principals to sign up for the date that works best for their school. Putting out the schedule in advance, during the summer or early August, ensures that everyone will schedule around the visit and makes it a priority for the central office administrator. Prior to the visit the central office administrator will review the school's SIP feedback so that during the visit issues identified are discussed.

Once on site the central office administrator meets with the principal to review SIP feedback and discuss the focus for the walkthrough. The principal determines which of their school's look fors will be targeted. During the walkthrough the central office administrator and the principal walk through the school, examining student work, talking to students, and observing in classrooms. It is important to get to as many classrooms as possible, but if unable to get to all classrooms the principal needs to determine which departments or wings of the school need to be observed. After walking through the school there is a debriefing. The debriefing offers an opportunity to deepen reflections through dialogue. The central office administrator asks open-ended questions that promote analysis from the principal. The purpose of the debriefing is to make sure that the principal can identify effective implementation efforts and identify next steps that address areas of concern. By asking open-ended questions the central office administrator can discern if the principal has a firm grasp on the current reality of the school. The purpose is not to browbeat the principal or point out deficit areas; rather the purpose is to support the principal and provide assistance so the principal has a clear picture of what is working and what next steps are in order to address areas of need (growth mindset).

After the supervisory walkthrough, principals write a letter to their staff that includes reflection on the visit. Typically, this letter includes quotes from the central office administrator that validate effective practices observed. The central office administrator reviews the letter prior to sending out to all staff in order to provide suggestions or feedback. The central office administrator may also want to provide feedback via a letter. This should occur after the central office administrator has completed a round of walkthroughs at a certain level. For example, after conducting walkthroughs in all middle schools, the central office administrator would write a letter to all middle school principals validating the teaching and learning practices that meet district goals. This type of feedback helps principals develop a deeper understanding of district goals and provides a model for giving feedback. An example of a supervisory feedback letter is found in Appendix E.

The central office leader uses the data collected during supervisory walkthroughs to help principals maintain a focus on school improvement efforts. The central office leader identifies patterns and trends across the system, helping to discover if principals have both enough content knowledge (understanding of the strategy and what it means when implemented) and process knowledge (understanding of the processes and facilitation skills necessary to move the school forward) to implement strategies in their plans. For example, if the district initiative was to utilize formative assessment data to respond to student needs, then a principal would need to have a deep understanding of effective formative assessment practices (content) *and* be able to facilitate the use and analysis of the data via PLCs (process). The central office leader needs to be attuned to these needs and make sure that the professional development plan developed (see Chapter 7, Spring) is addressing any gaps or misconceptions. Just as the building principal will adjust professional development based on implementation studies and walkthroughs, so must central office. Leading a school is complex work and principals need support. Providing professional learning opportunities based on the context of the district and school initiatives is a key element to principal support.

Move 2: Use Weekly Communication to Principals to Reinforce District Initiatives

Central office administration needs to adopt the common practice in many school buildings of sending a weekly message to staff. The weekly message from central office sent to principals should include nuts and bolts items, but more importantly it needs to reinforce the teaching and learning initiatives of the organization. By sharing thoughts and reflections on teaching and learning practices observed throughout the week, providing excerpts from articles that reinforce district-adopted best practices, and revisiting the district's mission, the central office administrator is conveying what matters most in the organization. Nuts and bolts items need to be addressed, but if all that is ever discussed is textbook orders or deadlines, these issues will take precedence over the real work of schools—teaching and learning.

By sharing ideas and thoughts on teaching and learning issues, the central office leader is not only shaping the organization's improvement efforts, but also allowing staff to get a better understanding of the leader. It is impossible to be in every school as much as one would like, so the weekly message gives the central office leader a "voice," helping them to develop relationships with the principals they supervise. When Ann was responsible for sixty elementary schools one of the first things she did was institute the "Mausbach Message." This was one of the first opportunities that principals had to understand who Ann was as a leader and to discuss the teaching and learning issues in the district. An example of the types of "thought for the week" included in every communication to principals can be found in Appendix F.

When Ann started writing her weekly messages they were attached to emails, but fortunately we now have more sophisticated tools at our fingertips. A Google site that included a blog was found to be the most effective method for communicating this information. The blog provided two-way communication, allowing for more dialogue with all of the principals. Other keys to successful implementation of a weekly message include:

- *Be relentless.* Publish *every* week. It is the ongoing communication that makes a difference in helping principals stay the course. Ann made sure that the message went out on the same day every week, even when it moved to a blog, in order to provide consistency and to help principals manage their busy schedules. Updating the message on Wednesday or Thursday was found to be most beneficial to principals, as many times they used information from the message in their weekly communications to staff, which typically went out on Friday.

- *Don't forget the nuts and bolts items.* It is important to include nuts and bolts items in the message so that when meeting with principals face-to-face for professional learning, valuable time isn't wasted on these items. Principal meetings should be devoted 100 percent to their learning. Including nuts and bolts items in the weekly message allows this to happen.

- *Make it a one-stop shop.* The weekly message should be the one-stop shop for the building leaders' communication needs. Rather than have every department bombard principals with emails that contain deadlines and notices, incorporate this information in the message. In large districts this can be extremely challenging, but in mid-size districts it can easily be achieved. If the goal of central office is to provide support to principals, leaders at this level must stop making their jobs more difficult. Providing clear and consistent information that is located in one spot is a simple practice that communicates to building principals that their time matters.

Have to Do: Develop Teachers by Responding to Individual Student Needs

Relationships are strengthened through working together to address teaching and learning issues (Robinson, 2011). There is no better example of this concept in action than the leader's commitment to providing a system of support for students. Having a system in place that recognizes what's successful and what's not working well leads to excellence (Studer, 2003). Effective leaders do this by creating a culture of evidence-based inquiry and improvement. A critical feature in this type of environment is using data to make individual and collaborative decisions regarding quality in both what students need to learn and how students need to learn, and the administrative and organizational supports necessary to do this teaching (Robinson, 2011). Teachers need to be able to explicitly guide students through systematic and intentional instruction and intervention. They need to continually monitor their efforts both in the moment and through analysis of student work in order to determine if instruction and intervention strategies are working. Leaders need to support teachers in observing students' responsiveness to targeted interventions and help them make decisions based on these observations and other evidence of student learning.

This type of environment is not created by treating intervention as a separate part of the work of the school. As well intentioned as the Response to Intervention (RtI) movement has been, it has created another silo, viewed all too frequently as a program, not an instructional mindset. The authors worked in a state where the Department of Education changed from calling the intervention process RtI to MTSS (multi-tiered system of support), resulting in much upheaval. Principals and teachers across the state felt they needed new training and had wasted time in implementing RtI and had to start over. This exemplifies how educators view intervention as a "project," not a way of thinking and behaving that is inherent in the teaching and learning cycle.

Helping teachers provide targeted supports to individual students requires leaders to create a foundation of support that is embedded in the daily work of the school. Intervening and responding to students' need becomes "just the way we do business" instead of another program required by higher ups. Inherent in this system is a mindset of blanketed support—giving a student everything they need when it is needed. All too often support for struggling students operates in a stair-step manner, trying one thing and if that fails abandoning that approach, moving to the next more restrictive level, until students end up in special education. The system of supports must be layered so that students can receive as many supports as needed simultaneously. Many times this means that supports need to exist both in the regular classroom and also in small group intervention outside of the classroom. There is a plethora of books available on this topic and it is outside the scope of this book to provide specificity around effective systems of support. *Enhancing RtI* by Fisher and Frey (2010) is a good place to start if guidance is needed. The key here for leaders is to make sure that a system is in place and that teachers have *ongoing* support on using quality instruction both in the regular classroom and in the intervention setting. Providing job-embedded time so collaborative problem solving can occur allows teams to use student work as the lens for monitoring and responding to individual needs.

Reflective Questions

Development Stage

- Has time been designated in the schedule for collaboration?
- Are layers of support identified for students who struggle?
- What will ongoing support to teachers look like?

Refinement Stage

- What evidence do we have that the interventions in place are working?
- Do teachers have the training they need to deliver interventions both in the classroom and in specialized settings?
- Are processes and procedures in place that allow teams to consistently look at and respond to student work?

Principal Move

Move: Use PLCs to Support Students and Teachers

The most effective and well researched way for leaders to support teachers in responding to student needs is through the Professional Learning Community (PLC) process (Blanton & Perez, 2011; Dufour, 2003; Fullan, 2001; Fullan & Hargreaves, 1996). PLCs, when focused on student work, create a community committed to addressing the individual needs of students. Principals may be lulled into thinking that they have PLCs because they designated time in the schedule for teachers to meet and collaborate. However, the principal's role in this process goes beyond logistics; leaders must be intimately involved if PLCs are going to have an impact. Principals do this by defining parameters for teachers' work in the PLC and by being an active participant. The principal's role is to lead teachers to improve their teaching, while learning alongside of them about what works and what doesn't; using the small group structure of PLCs is an effective way to make this happen. This involvement isn't about micro managing; rather it is about the leader developing the group by creating a collective culture of efficacy (Fullan, 2014).

Identifying supports for students with the most complex needs is difficult work that requires a skillful instructional leader who can facilitate the intricacies of this type of conversation. Diagnosing and responding to students who learn differently requires all hands on deck to identify effective interventions. The authors recommend that principals are an active participant in every PLC in the school at a minimum of once a week. Regular participation in and follow-up with PLCs embodies the leader's commitment to developing teachers and also to promoting a healthy culture. If regular routines for PLCs are established and followed, with a defined structure, the principal's role becomes more of a participant, allowing teacher leaders to emerge. When principals work alongside staff to problem-solve on student issues, trust is developed, which helps in building a student-centered culture.

The following practices aid the principal in committing to the work of PLCs:

1. *Schedule time on teachers' and the principal's calendar.* Make sure that blocks of time are scheduled within the school day for collaboration so teams can meet at least once a week. Identify when the principal will be in attendance at these meetings and keep this time sacred, scheduling other meetings and events around PLC times. Just as the practice of conducting walkthroughs needs to take priority on the leader's schedule, so does PLC time. If principals fail to attend these meetings, or do so on an infrequent basis, they will be unable to support teachers and will be disconnected from the ongoing discussions and learning taking place in the PLC. PLCs can become disjointed and run like meetings if processes and protocols aren't in place; see Appendix A for an example of a PLC agenda template. Having the principal regularly attend these meetings helps keep the focus on student supports and provides the leaders with deep insights into the learning needs of teachers.

2. *Collaboratively develop defined outcomes for every PLC meeting.* PLCs must have a purpose and a stated outcome for every meeting. A clearly defined purpose helps keep the group focused and helps to ensure that time spent in these learning teams results in changes in classroom practices. It isn't until teachers see how this time directly relates to or supports them with the teaching and learning issues faced in their

classroom that they will see the value of this practice. This won't happen without a clear outcome and accompanying plan for the learning time. Starting every meeting with the outcome and ending with a summary and focus for the next meeting time is a critical feature of high impact, high functioning teams. The principal needs to help support these outcomes by providing learning resources during team time, asking probing questions that help the team think richly about the issue, and summarizing and clarifying when there are misconceptions. Having a common structure for PLC time helps utilize the time most efficiently and helps create a rhythm to the work. For example, Kim's PLC structure always follows this same pattern. First the meeting starts with revisiting norms, and a warm-up activity around the mission that answers questions like "What is our fundamental purpose, what do we value and how do we know?" Using Dufour, Dufour, Eaker, and Many's (2006) essential questions as the overarching target, guided questions that aim at providing more specificity help focus the team on a defined outcome. Resources and data are then reviewed in order to answer the guiding question for the meeting. Once the question is answered, teachers plan how to respond to the data in practical terms in their classrooms. Finally, teachers leave the meeting by answering the question, "What have you accomplished during this PLC to respond to student achievement?" This predictable routine helps to ensure that the work is focused on students and isn't dependent on the principal leading the group.

3. *Use progress monitoring data for students and teachers.* Progress monitoring evaluates the effectiveness of interventions and allows teachers to respond to students' needs. The key to progress monitoring is to not only collect the data, but to use it to help inform instruction. The principal needs to make sure that formative data being collected on students is used to answer the question "Is learning taking place?" Standard processes for data collection and retrieval need to be in place so PLC time can be spent on identifying practices to respond to the data. This data may be as formal as district common assessments or as simple as a checklist developed for a unit of study by the team. It's not so much about the assessment as it is about the use of the assessment. Does the team know if core instruction and interventions are working? If not, what needs to happen next? Many times this results in the need for a focused walkthrough in order to help answer this question. The

data from focused walkthroughs helps the team pinpoint effective practices. Data is the fuel for effective PLC work.

4. *Use protocols to analyze student work.* A critical tool for leaders when working in PLCs is protocols that allow for analysis of student work. Protocols are a structured process or set of guidelines devised to promote meaningful and effective communication (Southern Maine Partnership). Analyzing student work is difficult for teachers, especially at first, as they may feel guarded, defensive, and vulnerable. The structured nature of a protocol helps build trust because it provides a predictable organization to reviewing student work and keeps the lens on the learning. Protocols allow all members of a group to have equal input, promoting skills necessary in a collaborative culture.

5. *Make sure to include all "knowledgeable others."* A "more knowledgeable other" is someone, according to Vygotsky (1962), who is perceived to have more knowledge or skill to perform a certain task. There are many knowledgeable others in schools who need to be called upon when collaborating on student learning needs. Instructional coaches, mentors, interventionists, and special education specialists need to be tapped to participate in PLCs on a regular basis to help support learning interventions in the regular classroom and to connect strategies learned outside of the regular classroom.

Central Office Moves

 ### *Move 1: Provide Infrastructure of Support by Defining Quality*

Successful school systems have high internal accountability that means that there is high agreement around values and an organizational scheme that make values evident in practice (Elmore, 2008). The central office administrator influences internal coherence and accountability through the process of defining quality for organizational strategies. When it comes to meeting the individual needs of students, defining quality requires central office staff to identify what the standards will be for intervention systems and the process that supports building level collaboration (i.e., PLCs).

Table 6.4 District Questions for Intervention System

• What are the layers of support for students?
• Do the layers of support look different at different levels (elementary, middle, high)?
• How will the intervention systems for literacy, math, and behavior be alike and different?
• Who will deliver interventions outside of the regular education classroom?
• How do general education teachers receive training on classroom interventions?
• How will specialists receive ongoing training on interventions?
• What common methodologies will be used to monitor progress of students in specialized interventions?

In order to identify standards for intervention, central office administrators need to focus less time on figuring out the mandated accountability system and more time on using the accountability system to position the organization to gain resources and develop capacity (Elmore, 2008). This is achieved by working in district level teams to learn about and eventually develop a system of support. Identifying a common vision, terminology, and best practices provides clarity and aids in the strategic use of resources. Shared meaning across the organization around the intervention system increases internal accountability and provides central office staff with mechanisms to monitor and respond to building needs. Table 6.4 identifies questions that district teams need to answer when developing an intervention system.

The second aspect of defining quality at the district level focuses on ensuring that all teams in every school in the district are working from a common framework for collaboration. Clearly establishing what should occur during collaborative meeting times and identifying expected outcomes increases internal accountability and helps to make certain that this powerful process has real impact on student results. The fact that teachers have time in their schedules to collaborate does not guarantee true collaboration or improvement. Improved results can only be accomplished if the professionals engaged in the collaboration are focused on the right things (Dufour, Dufour, Eaker, & Many, 2006). While all schools in Ann's district had collaboration time embedded in schedules and were reporting that PLCs were firmly in place, achievement results were not on target. After further investigation and observation it was evident that while time was being carved out of schedules for collaboration, far too often this time was not spent on identifying student learning targets, collecting and analyzing student work, or responding to student needs. Internal coherence was needed, so the PLC process was "rebooted" and rebranded as Learning Teams, with clear training on the phases of this work and desired outcomes. Table 6.5 provides an outline of the process that was implemented across the district. Defining the organizational scheme for this process allowed central office personnel to support building principals through observations of team meetings and providing feedback on products developed during meetings, dramatically increasing internal capacity, which resulted in improved student outcomes.

 ## Move 2: Distribute Resources Strategically

The challenge for district level administrators is to allocate available resources so they have the greatest impact on student results. The building leader is one of the district's most valuable assets, second only to teachers in terms of impact on student results, and as such consideration should be given to how they spend their time (Robinson, Lloyd, & Rowe, 2008). Central office administrators need to be as vigilant about protecting time spent on teaching and learning by building principals as principals need to be about protecting teachers' instructional time. This means that central office needs to be strategic about the amount of time that the building principal is out of the building attending professional development or meetings. One method for doing this is to make sure that all district level trainings and meetings occur on the same day of the week. For example, district level meetings are only held on Wednesdays. This means that building leaders can plan collaborative learning team meetings around this day, making sure not to hold PLCs on that specific day of the week. Another method is through the weekly communication described in Chapter 5. District level leaders need to be cognizant of the time they are pulling principals away from their most important work, leading teaching and learning in the building. With forethought and coordination, disruptions can be minimal.

Table 6.5 Learning Team Cycle

PHASE 1: PLANNING—*What do we want students to learn?*
• **Product: Learning Targets ("I Can" Statements . . .)** Develop and/or clarify meaning for each Power grade level expectation for each unit of study. This can include specific Learning Targets and/or "I Can" Statements for each GLE. *Do these reflect what you're spending a majority of your time teaching?*
• **Product: Proficiency Statements** Create Proficiency Statements for each Learning Target and/or "I Can" Statement. *Do these reflect proficient and non-proficient descriptors of student outcomes/work?*
• **Product: SMART Goals** Develop a SMART Goal based on Learning Targets and/or "I Can" Statements based on Proficiency Statements.
PHASE 2: IMPLEMENTATION—*How do we know if students are learning?*
• **Product: Formative Assessment** Collaboratively develop Formative Assessments related to each Learning Target/"I Can" Statement and guided by Proficiency Statements to evaluate student learning.
• **Product: Analysis of Student Work** Collaboratively score Formative Assessments using Proficiency Statements and utilize the Data Dig protocol for analysis and identify strengths and weaknesses in student learning.
• **Product: Results** As Formative Assessments and District Assessments are given, analyze the data.
PHASE 3: ACTION—*What do we do when students learn/do not learn?*
• **Product: Action Plan** Utilize your results to create a plan of action for both struggling and advancing learners. *What happens if kids don't learn? Do we know each student's level of mastery and those that need more time and support? What is our plan for reteaching and challenging these students?*
Repeat Process. Remember, this is a cyclical process that occurs no less than once per unit. **Expectations for Learning Teams:** • Meet weekly • Includes principal and/or assistant principal • Grouped by grade level (elementary) or common course (secondary) • Submit Learning Team Log each week.

Strategic resourcing requires the central office leader to allocate resources based on student needs. This means that not every building will get the same amount of resources. Student data is the driver for resource allocation, not building size, or location. Support services don't always have to be assigned to schools, but rather to students. For example, if the district has an intensive one-on-one intervention for early readers, these highly trained specialists can be "rovers" in the district who at mid-year review data to determine if students have made significant progress and can be exited, and to identify students who may have moved in with even greater needs. Assignments shift at this time so that students who are struggling the most have access to the most highly qualified teachers. Central office staff need to have processes and procedures in place that allow for mid-year checks in regard to student intervention systems in order to ensure that resource allocations are meeting student needs across the system.

Have to Do: Embed the Mission in the Work

Time spent on mission and vision development and revision in the fall will be for naught if processes for spotlighting the mission throughout the year are not in place. The winter can be a bleak time in the cycle of a school year. The excitement of the new year has worn off for both teachers and students and the challenges of meeting all students' needs can be daunting. There is no better time to recall, revisit, and reinforce the mission in action than during the winter months. Embedding the mission into the daily work of the school helps create alignment between beliefs and actions. When the going gets tough, and it more than likely will in these months, the leader needs to harken back to purpose. Providing evidence that what we do matches what we say we will do increases an organization's integrity. Integrity, according to the dictionary, is the state of being whole or undivided. One of the tenets of system leadership is to make the system whole by setting direction to enable all learners to reach their potential and to translate vision into a whole school curriculum with consistency and high expectations (Leithwood, Day, Sammons, Harris, & Hopkins, 2006). Referring to the mission, vision, values, and beliefs of the organization helps to provide consistency and focus in the school or system.

Leaders must take every opportunity to review and find evidence of the mission in action. It is the filter for examining student work and it is the driver for teacher behaviors. Every time staff come together, learning the mission should serve as a warm-up. Teachers and principals should be asked to cite evidence from their work or that of others that indicates implementation of the mission or a value statement. This type of warm-up takes less than 5 minutes and renews commitment to the mission.

Reflective Questions

Development Stage

● What processes do you have in place to recall, revisit, and reinforce the mission?

● What evidence will you collect to demonstrate the school is living by the mission?

Refinement Stage

● Were the processes in place to recall, revisit, and reinforce the mission effective?

● What evidence exists to demonstrate the school is living by the mission?

Principal Move

Move: Use the Mission as a Lens for Revising and Adopting New Initiatives

If an activity or a professional development practice cannot directly align to the mission it shouldn't be implemented. There simply isn't enough time in the school year to waste. Teachers often have excellent ideas that they would like to implement, but doing so may take the school in an unwanted direction. The mission serves as the guidepost for goal setting. Goal setting works because it reduces fragmentation and promotes coherence. There are many important things that need to happen in schools; the purpose of setting goals isn't about determining what is important and not important. The purpose and beauty of goal setting is that it forces decisions about what is important in the context of the school at that moment in time (Robinson, 2011). The principal must make sure that all activities are in alignment with the mission and goals, and their job is to help teachers see this alignment. For example, if the school's philosophy of discipline is based on Ross Greene's Problem Solving Approach (2008) because it aligns to the school's mission and goals, it would be inappropriate to send a group of teachers to workshops on Assertive Discipline. Using the mission and goals of the school as the lens for decision-making helps keep focus on the important things in the context of the particular school related to their progress at a certain point in time.

Central Office Move

 ### *Move: Reinforce Importance of Mission with Principals through Reflective Practice*

Central office administrators should model the importance of mission by using the district's mission, vision, values, and goals throughout the year and in a variety of communications with building leaders. While these practices are important, the most critical thing the central office leader can do is to help building principals become reflective practitioners. According to Schon (1987), reflective practice requires the ability to reflect in action and on action. The ability to analyze and think about a problem when you are in the midst of it is reflection in action; reflection on action occurs after the fact; both are important and are related. The better a leader gets at reflection *on* action translates to improvement on reflection *in* action. Opportunities to slow down and think can, unfortunately, be rare in the course of a busy school day. Thus, it is imperative that the central office administrator provides opportunities for reflection on action to occur on a regular basis. One way this is achieved is by organizing learning teams within the principal ranks. This means having the same small groups of principals work together each month as part of their professional develop-ment time. Providing reflective questions centered on the core values and mission of the district and schools can help leaders, working in their learning teams, see their place in the system and learn from each other. Examples of the types of reflective questions asked of principals include:

- Where do you want your school to be at this time next year?

- What actions do you need to take now to get there?

- What do you notice have been "hits" in terms of meeting your mission? What have been "misses"?

- What are the strongest artifacts that exist in your school that demonstrate the mission in action? What artifacts do you wish you had, but currently don't?

Summary

The winter months are when the seeds of improvement take root. Leaders' commitments to school improvement, a healthy culture, and developing teachers are manifested in the way the school improvement plan is monitored, how individual students are supported through the PLC process, and how the mission is embedded in daily actions. In combination, these actions by all leaders in the system work together to yield higher results for students.

Planting a Seed: If You Say You Can . . . You Are Right!

Tinkerbell is a character who is known for her difficult diva nature. She can be precocious, moody, helpful, exciting, and in the end wonderfully rewarding. In the story of Peter Pan, Tinkerbell was dying and, in order to save her, everyone needed to wish and say aloud, "I do believe! I do believe!" and she came to life.

Our school improvement process and progress can feel like this. We work so hard to put forth our best efforts in lesson planning, explicit language, kind words, etc., and then boom, someone or something will slam your confidence. It could be bumps in student behavior, motivation, or lower than expected performance that will make you feel like screaming! It is through our relentless focus that we persevere.

As we continue to work on meaningful engagement, here is what some of your colleagues have said effective constructive learning looks like in practice:

Students can explain purpose of lesson and apply it to their own learning in becoming a self-regulated learner. Students don't need guidance in behavior norms because they are so excited and focused investigating.

Evidence of student thinking will be evident . . . abundance of student work will be available because the students were so focused and understood the relevance of the learning in the real world.

Students will be engaged and remember new learning for guided practice and be able to apply that new learning.

Clearly, many of our staff members understand rigor and are implementing these concepts in their instruction. Know you can make a difference and you will. We are 82 percent proficient in reading comprehension! The data wall indicates 78 percent at or above grade level in reading. The students have the ability; let's provide rigorous expectations so they can show us what they've got!

Remember belief is key.

References

Blanton, L. P., & Perez, Y. (2011, March). Exploring the relationship between special education teachers and professional learning communities: Implications of research for administrators. *Journal of Special Education Leadership*, 24 (1), 6–16.

Dufour, R. (2003). Building a professional learning community. *School Administrator*, 60 (5), 13–18.

Dufour, R., Dufour, R., Eaker, R., & Many, T. (2006). *Learning by doing: A handbook for professional learning communities at work*. Bloomington, IN: Solution Tree.

Elmore, R. (2008). Leadership as the practice of improvement. In Pont, B., Nusche, D., & Hopkins, D. (Eds.), *Improving school leadership, volume 2: Case studies on system leadership* (pages 13–35), 2nd ed. Paris: Organisation for Economic Co-operation and Development.

Fisher, D., & Frey, N. (2010). *Enhancing RtI: How to ensure success with effective classroom instruction and intervention*. Alexandria, VA: ASCD.

Fisher, D., & Frey, N. (2013). *Better learning through structured teaching: A framework for the gradual release of responsibility*, 2nd ed. Alexandria, VA: ASCD.

Fullan, M. (2001). *Leading in a culture of change*. San Francisco, CA: Jossey-Bass.

Fullan, M. (2014). *The principal: Three keys to maximizing impact*. San Francisco, CA: Jossey-Bass.

Fullan, M., & Hargreaves, A. (1996). *What's worth fighting for in your school?* New York: Teachers College Press.

Greene, R. W. (2008). *Lost at school: Why our kids with behavioral challenges are falling through the cracks and how we can help them*. New York: Scribner.

Leithwood, K., Day, C., Sammons, P., Harris, A., & Hopkins, D. (2006). *Seven strong claims about successful school leadership*. Nottingham: National College for School Leadership/Department of Education and Skills.

Louis, K. S., Leithwood, K., Wahlstrom, K., & Anderson, S. (2010) *Learning from leadership: Investigating the links to improved student learning*. Seattle: Center for Applied Research and Educational Improvement, University of Minnesota; and Toronto: Ontario Institute for Studies in Education, University of Toronto.

Marshall, K. (2013). *Rethinking teacher supervision and evaluation: How to work smart, build collaboration, and close the achievement gap*, 2nd ed. San Francisco, CA: Jossey-Bass.

Robinson, V. M. (2011). *Student centered leadership*. San Francisco, CA: Jossey-Bass.

Robinson, V. M. J., Lloyd, A., & Rowe, J. (2008). The impact of leadership on student outcomes: An analysis of the different effects of leadership styles. *Educational Administration Quarterly*, 44 (5), 635–674.

Schon, D. A. (1987). *Educating the reflective practitioner: A new design for teaching and learning in the professions*. San Francisco, CA: Jossey-Bass.

Sizer, T. (2004). *Horace's compromise: The dilemma of the American high school*. New York: Mariner Books.

Southern Maine Partnership. A rationale for protocols. www.schoolreforminitiative. org/download/Documents%20to%20Support%20the%20use%20of%20Protocol s/rationale_for_protocols.pdf

Stringer, E. T. (2007). *Action research*, 3rd ed. Thousand Oaks, CA: Sage Publishers.

Studer, Q. (2003). *Hardwiring excellence: Purpose, worthwhile work, making a difference*. Gulf Breeze, FL: Fire Starter Publishing.

Vygotsky, L. S. (1962). *Thought and language*. Cambridge, MA: MIT Press. (Original work published in 1934).

Spring
Staying the Course While Looking Forward

A good garden may have some weeds.

Thomas Fuller

Pulling weeds is a natural part of gardening. Getting rid of unwanted weeds is not just an exercise in aesthetics, but a vital aspect to a bountiful garden. Weeds steal nutrients and space that belong to healthy plants and if left to their own devices will take over the garden. Seasoned gardeners understand that weeding, while a chore, is essential to the long-term well-being of the garden. Expert gardeners attack this task with a clear vision for the type of garden they desire. Dandelions, for example, may be pulled from a flower-bed, but would be welcome in an herb garden. The steady work of removing the roots of the weeds ensures that the mainstay of the garden, plants, have all of the nutrients they need to thrive.

The spring season for school leaders requires a focus on the health and well-being of the school or district. The vision and direction for the school that was planted in the fall and nurtured in the winter needs to continue, with an eye on making sure that any distractions or unproductive practices are eliminated. School leaders need to make decisions in the spring to determine if school improvement efforts have been successful and if staff have the support they need to continue to grow. They need to weed out the processes that are standing in the way of the continued development of a healthy culture that results in higher levels of achievement for students. The "have to dos" in the spring include:

- Have to Do: Stay the course while planning ahead.
- Have to Do: Support professional learning.
- Have to Do: Recognize improvement.

Have to Do: Stay the Course While Planning Ahead

Ann vividly remembers teaching her oldest son to drive. The first time he tried driving on the Interstate Ann offered him three pieces of advice. (This was of course after asking him to turn down the music so he could hear her.) First, she reminded him that he had to maintain a reasonable speed. If he went too fast he would be out of control, and if he went too slow he could get rear-ended. Second, she told him that he needed to make sure to look behind him. This was essential if he was going to be able to move over before the lane merged. Finally, she advised him to make sure that he also kept his eye on the windshield so he didn't inadvertently hit the car ahead of him. And of course he had to do these things simultaneously with both hands firmly planted on the steering wheel.

During the spring administrators have one foot planted in the current year and the other in the upcoming year, much like a driver merging into traffic. There are three keys to successfully navigating this time of the year.

1. *Maintain a reasonable speed.* Spring is not the time to shut down. There is still a significant amount of instructional time left in the year. Keep students engaged in high-level tasks. Don't waste one student's time by showing movies and doing artsy crafty projects that masquerade as learning. Spring is also not the time to speed up. It goes without saying that adding any new initiatives at this point in the year is a bad idea.

2. *Look behind you.* This is the time of year when both impact and implementation data around the school improvement plan should be reviewed. What does this data mean? Identify the things that worked to keep the team focused on goals, and move or modify the efforts that didn't keep the school on the right track.

3. *Look ahead.* Revisit the collaboratively shared vision for the school. Does everyone in the school know where you are headed? How will your school look different at this time next year and what steps do you need to take to make that happen?

It's so easy to get distracted during the spring with end-of-year celebrations, changes in staffing, parent programs, etc. Leaders can turn down the noise and keep both hands steady on the wheel, arriving at the end of the year with the desired results, by attending to the moves in this chapter.

Reflective Questions

Development Stage

- What processes do you have in place to collect data on school improvement efforts?
- What are you learning about your school from the data you have collected on strategy implementation from your school improvement plan?
- How will you maintain focus during this time of year?

Refinement Stage

- Is the data being collected on the school improvement plan useful in helping to monitor progress on implementation and student growth?
- What revisions need to be made to the school improvement plan for next year based on this year's data?

Principal Moves

Move 1: Monitor Instruction

Educators across the United States lament the loss of instructional time due to state accountability testing. While this debate rages on, the immediate concern for educators must be how to most effectively utilize the instructional time that currently exists. Research has shown that increasing the time available for learning (i.e., increasing the length of the school day or year) is not likely to be productive unless the time is used to engage students in learning (Blai, 1986). Maximizing academic learning time, defined as instructional time when learning is taking place, is related to increases in academic achievement and is what matters most in the current debate on time (Aronson, Zimmerman, & Carlos, 1998). It may seem hypocritical to some for educators to decry the loss of instructional time and spend the last months of school squandering this precious commodity.

During the spring the principal needs to make sure that students are still learning. The walkthrough and feedback processes described in earlier chapters become critical at this time of year. Teachers shouldn't waste students' time by having them do busy work that neither extends nor reinforces learning. Showing an 8- to 10-minute movie clip to illustrate a point, or going on a field trip to extend classroom learning, are appropriate practices that should be occurring. However, during the spring, showing full-length movies or going on a field trip because it is a rite of passage abuses these effective practices. There needs to be a reciprocal relationship for honoring the precious commodity of time in school for both teachers and students. Leaders honor students' time by being vigilant, keeping their eye on the school improvement plan, observing in classrooms, and providing feedback.

Move 2: Benchmark Progress on School Improvement Efforts

A lack of results on external measures doesn't indicate that progress is not being made in the school. Staff in the school may be working hard at implementing new instructional practices but haven't yet reached a level that allows them to freely replace previously used less effective practices with newly acquired ones. As previously stated, school improvement is a developmental process, and as such is not linear in progression, but more a series of starts and stops. Elmore (2008) explains this phenomenon as a seesaw relationship between key variables. One variable advances before another one can: the latter variable moves, while the former stays constant or declines. Two key variables in the school improvement process are quality and external performance measures. Typically quality precedes improvement on external performance measures. Improvement in achievement on state accountability measures happens *after* improvements in instructional practice are solidly in place. What this means in practice is that substantial changes to instructional practice can occur in a school, but the external measures of performance may stay the same or even decline. Teachers must have competence with the new instructional practice in order to replace ineffective practices. This competence is developed over time after lots of teaching at a relatively high level. Once this is achieved, results in external performance measures improve. A misunderstanding of the inherent seesaw nature of school improvement processes results in schools abandoning practices too soon.

Leaders who understand the systematic nature of school improvement processes monitor both implementation (quality) and impact (internal performance) data in order to determine the effectiveness of their efforts. External performance measures serve as markers for long-term goals, but it is the ongoing attention paid to changes in student learning through-out the year that guides day-to-day actions. Each strategy in the school improvement plan should have clearly identified measures that help a school team determine effectiveness and next steps. Table 7.1 provides an example of the implementation and impact data collected for a literacy strategy in a school improvement plan.

Implementation data helps the leader answer the question, "Is the strat-egy being implemented with fidelity?" Impact data answers the question, "Has implementation made a difference?" The straightforward nature of these questions can mislead the leader into thinking that improving a school is a simple input-output equation. Finding the answers to these important questions is like a waltz rather than a line dance. A leader will sometimes feel like they are taking two steps back and one step forward as they hypothesize, observe, investigate, and analyze information. The back and forth of this process can be illustrated in an example from the work of an elementary principal who had the goal of increasing proficiency in reading and math. The strategy identified to meet this goal was to respond with appropriate instruction at the individual, small group, and whole group level by using and monitoring acquisition of learning targets. One of the first data points the principal collected was whether students could state the learning target of the lesson. Data indicated that students clearly under-stood learning targets for mathematics, but had difficulty stating targets for reading. Impact data from common assessments that measured common core standards showed limited mastery in reading, while again math data looked stronger. Armed with this information the principal conducted focused walkthroughs during the reading block. Through these observations and the work in PLCs the principal determined that teachers weren't

Table 7.1 SIP—Impact and Implementation Data Example

Strategy: Implement tailored instruction using formative data to accelerate student growth. Evidence of strategy implementation:	
Impact Data	Implementation Data

• District assessments
  – Subgroups: Movement & Gap analysis
  – Standard analysis
• Data wall
  – Subgroups: Movement & Gap analysis
  – Overall proficiency
• IA skills data
  – Subgroups: Movement & Gap analysis
  – Standard analysis
• Tier 1 data
  – % of students exiting intervention
  – Growth percentage
• IA assessments
  – Overall proficiency
  – Subgroups
  – NPR
	• % of student-friendly learning targets articulated by students
	• Teacher-created tools to monitor progress and to collect data toward standards and learning targets
	• Organized Tier 1 intervention schedule
	• Shared action steps to respond to common formative assessments
	• Data dig results identifying mastered and non-mastered standards
	• Formative assessments created in PLCs

teaching during guided (small group) instruction and that conferring with students one-on-one was rarely occurring, even though in the previous year staff had received considerable training in these areas. Knowing that students needed these supports the principal used whole group professional development time to help staff develop a deeper understanding of what guided practice and conferring should look like in literacy. This learning resulted in the staff restructuring the literacy block so that richer opportunities for small group and one-on-one instruction could occur. After a month of utilizing the new structure, implementation data indicated staff had increased the amount of time they were working in small group instruction and conferring, yet impact data indicated there was little evidence that it was making a difference for student learning. Again the principal conducted focused walkthroughs, and identified two areas of concern: staff needed help understanding how to teach the standards and they needed support with how to respond when students didn't learn. During PLC times the principal worked with staff to make sure that they understood what students needed to learn by unpacking standards and refining "I Can" statements. PLC time was also used to identify and model classroom interventions. After several months of focus on these issues, implementation and impact data in reading improved. The principal continued to provide support in these areas so improvement could be sustained, reinforcing the idea that focusing and monitoring implementation can positively influence achievement.

Data collection techniques do not need to be elaborate or cumbersome to benchmark progress. Data simply needs to provide proof that improvement efforts are making a difference. This requires that clear indicators are identified during plan development (fall) and monitored throughout the year. Table 7.2 is an example of a simple progress monitoring tool Kim used in google documents. During the spring the leader needs to take the time to reflect deeply on this data in order to help the leadership team determine which efforts have been successful and, for those that haven't, what are the next steps.

Central Office Move

Move: Identify and Communicate Instructional Focus for Upcoming Year

For many readers the wording of this move may cause a visceral reaction due to the top-down nature of the language. However, research on system change has taught us that the question about decision-making and control isn't about at what level, but *how* within and across levels (Honig, Copland, Rainey, Lorton, & Newton, 2010). Neither top-down nor bottom-up change work by themselves, they have to be in balance (Pont & Hopkins, 2008). Thus, central office leaders do not need to shy away from making system decisions as long as the process for doing so isn't in isolation from building level personnel and is based on data collected in context of the schools in the system.

Table 7.2 SIP Progress Monitoring Form Example

TEMPLATE

Teacher: Grade Level: Content:				
Date	**Look For**	**Look For: Implementation Data**	**Student Work: Impact Data**	**Environmental Artifacts**

Example

Teacher: Ms. J.
Grade Level: 6
Content: Language Arts

Date	**Look For**	**Look For: Implementation Data**	**Student Work: Impact Data**	**Environmental Artifacts**
4/22	Teacher scaffolds the tasks (prompts/cues/graphic organizers) allowing students to access a variety of levels of thinking on the revised taxonomy.	Teacher working with small group of students. She said, "Let's look at your chart. I noticed that you have determined the theme to be overcoming obstacles. Please show me in the text where you have found evidence to support this theme." The teacher prompted the student to a specific page and then did a 1- to 2-minute think-aloud and cued the student to cite the evidence.	Student proficiency chart rubric using comprehension rubric standards RL1, RL2, RL4, RL9: section 1: 65% section 2: 87% section 3: 72%	Co-constructed chart using language of the standard

Large-scale improvement occurs when a system has a tight instructional focus sustained over time (Elmore, 2004). It is the responsibility of central office staff in charge of teaching and learning to make sure that there is a clearly articulated instructional focus for the entire system. This is necessary for system coherence, but also for lateral capacity building, another essential principle for large-scale system reform (Fullan, 2010). Central to system coherence is identifying a focus that is neither too narrow nor too broad. A narrow focus results in prescribed reforms that leave staff feeling disgruntled and disconnected. A broad focus results in ambiguity and confusion, or worse, claims that "we are already doing that," with no evidence to prove otherwise. The "just right" focus allows for enough definition to allow for widespread understanding and implementation, but is also open enough to allow for innovation within the framework. Figure 7.1 provides examples of district focus that are too tight, too loose, and "just right."

A "just right" focus is prey to being too broad if it isn't clearly defined. Central office staff in conjunction with building staff need to make sure that the focus is clearly defined. In addition, the following guidelines serve to help make sure the focus for the system is "just right":

- *Build on previous learning in the system.* Identifying a yearly focus doesn't mean doing something entirely different each year; this type of thinking results in what Reeves (2010) refers to as initiative fatigue. The

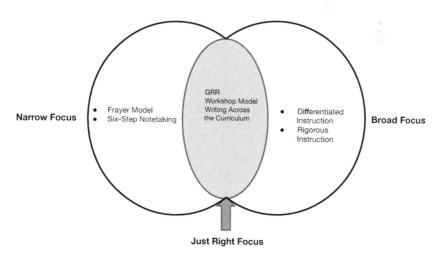

Just Right Focus

Figure 7.1 Examples of Narrow, Just Right, and Broad District Foci

yearly focus should be connected to previous learning in the district. For example, if a focus for the district was to use formative assessments to respond to student needs, after a year of implementation a district might determine that teachers need more support in providing classroom supports, so the focus for the upcoming year would be using additional classroom interventions. Or, to give another example, after a year of implementing the gradual release of responsibility, a district may decide that teachers need more support in using academic language; thus that would become the focus. These examples illustrate how the focus should be a refinement or extension of previous learning.

- *Use data.* Data collected both via district assessments and more importantly supervisory walkthroughs and coaching visits, needs to be used to determine focus. Observational data from classrooms across the district provides the context for this decision. After three years of implementing a workshop model at the elementary level, Ann's team conducted an implementation study that revealed teachers didn't understand how to scaffold supports to students via anchor charts and small group instruction, so this became a focus. Using data on current initiatives in the context of the classroom helps to ensure that the progression of learning continues, allowing the system to increase capacity and move from prescription to professionalism (Fullan, 2003).

- *Learn from the innovators.* The developmental nature of school improvement means that not all schools in the system will be at the same place at the same time. One of the critical reasons for identifying the "just right" focus is that it allows school teams who are further ahead in understanding and implementation to soar or innovate within the structure. Innovators work within the parameters of the system's structures, but improve upon or enhance the work. These improvements can serve as models for the next steps in system level implementation. For example, one principal who was concerned with meeting individual needs of students and aligning intervention supports started using a data wall to track student progress. After a successful year of implementation, data walls were required K–8.

- *Target process, not products.* The instructional focus should never be a program, but a process. Focusing on program implementation is a sure recipe for stalling improvement efforts because it relies on prescriptions rather than professional capital. This is not to say that districts won't be implementing resources to support curriculum implementation, but the instructional focus should not be derived from a canned program. The essence of the instructional focus is around helping teachers support students by improving instructional practice and that doesn't occur by following a script or six simple steps. It happens through learning and implementation.

One of the biggest benefits of having an instructional focus that is identified in the spring prior to a new year is that it eliminates surprises for staff and allows them time during the summer months to pursue learning around the focus. Another advantage is that it helps the central office leader say, "No!" Leaders at this level get bombarded with solicitations from professional organizations and salespeople promoting products and services. Many of the products or services may have great value, but aren't what the system needs at that specific point in time. Without a clear focus, district leaders are prey to purchasing these services, jeopardizing system coherence and sustainable reform efforts.

Have to Do: Support Professional Learning

Keeping learning at the center of the work is not just for the students at this time of year; adults also need to continue to learn and grow. During the spring, administrators need to continue to attend to the professional learning structures in the school, playing an active role, so staff can learn from each other in specific ways. Leaders who promote and *participate in* the professional learning and development of teachers have twice the impact on student outcomes (.84 effect size) of any other dimension identified in Robinson's (2011) research on student-centered leadership.

In order to keep professional learning on track during this busy time of year, leaders need to apply two important concepts. The first concept is the principle of reciprocity. In social psychology this means responding to action with another action. Applying this concept to professional development means that for every unit of performance that a leader requires of a teacher, the leader owes the teacher a unit of capacity to produce that result (Elmore, 2008). Leaders must avoid limiting, canceling, or failing to participate in professional growth opportunities in the spring. Improving student achievement results requires a firm commitment to adult learning and this can't waiver at this busy time of year.

The second critical concept is the importance of connecting adult learning as closely as possible to classroom practice. This means continuing to observe and use student work as the basis for learning so that teachers see the immediate application. The work of PLCs outlined in Chapter 6 needs to continue, and at this time of year the leader needs to critically appraise the outcomes from this work in order to determine if adjustments to practices are necessary. Observations and feedback collected throughout the year help the leader keep the focus on learning by providing valuable information on teacher development.

Reflective Questions

Development Stage

- What does the student work tell you about present levels of performance? Is student work the cornerstone of PLC work?
- Are the processes for PLCs being implemented with fidelity?
- What strategies do I need to have in place to ensure my participation in all professional learning?

Refinement Stage

- What does the student work and walkthrough feedback tell you about current levels of performance in your school?
- How effective is the work of PLCs?
- How will evidence from PLCs and walkthroughs inform teacher evaluations?
- Do I need to adjust strategies I have in place to ensure my participation in all professional learning?

Principal Moves

Move 1: Develop/Revisit Infrastructure for Professional Learning

Joyce and Showers' (1980) research on professional development structures, serves as the model for professional practice. These models result in deep levels of learning and build capacity. As people move from awareness to institutionalization of professional development practices, the types and structures of support must change. Figure 5.2 depicts the levels of support necessary, which, as previously mentioned, need to be offered in layers, providing multiple support structures. Not all staff will be at the same point on the continuum at the same time, which is one of the reasons why leaders stumble when it comes to leading professional learning. A one-dimensional approach will not get the job done, meaning an early release once a week that provides opportunities for large group and small group learning isn't enough. Principals need to identify and embed multiple small group learning times throughout the schedule to meet the diverse needs of staff and to address the varied needs of students in the school. Table 7.3 outlines team structures that have been effective in elementary and secondary settings. The small group structures in the school will vary based on the needs of the school and will evolve as school improvement processes mature.

Central to successful learning in PLCs is the leader's ability to develop a schedule that has this work ingrained in the culture of the school. Considerable forethought is needed for this to happen. Leaders need to spend time in the spring reviewing or revising the master schedule so that collaboration is a regular part of a teacher's day. Master scheduling at the secondary level can be extremely time-consuming, so it is essential that collaboration time is a part of the build for the schedule. At the elementary level it requires the principal, with input from staff, to develop a master schedule rather than having teachers individually determine their schedules and submit them to the office.

Table 7.3 Small Group Learning (PLCs) Opportunities

ELEMENTARY

Team Composition	Purpose	Frequency of Meeting Times
Grade level team: all teachers teaching the same grade, instructional coach	Identify what students need to learn, assess whether learning has occurred, and respond to students' learning	Once a week with principal
Inquiry team: all teachers who are interested in the same topic of study	Differentiate professional development and provide choice, based on individual teacher interests and school-wide goals	Once a week with or without principal
Planning team: all teachers in the same grade level and specialists who support instruction (coaches, mentors, etc.)	Develop lesson plans for the week	Minimum once a week without principal
Intervention team: Intervention teachers and classroom teachers	Identify and learn classroom interventions for struggling students	Once a month with principal

SECONDARY

Team Composition	Purpose	Frequency of Meeting Times
Content team: all teachers teaching the same content in the same grade (8th grade math)	Identify what students need to learn, assess whether learning has occurred, and respond to students' learning	Once a week with principal or assistant principal
Interdisciplinary team: all teachers who teach the same group of students	Provide support to students and coordinate instruction	Once a week with or without principal or assistant principal
Inquiry team: all teachers who are interested in the same topic of study	Differentiate professional development and provide choice, based on individual teacher interests and school-wide goals	Once a week with or without principal
Intervention team: Intervention teachers and classroom teachers	Identify and learn classroom interventions for struggling students	Once a month with principal

Move 2: Evaluate Staff Using Supervision Practices

Springtime is when most school districts require principals to complete evaluations on teachers using the district appraisal instrument. Crude appraisal systems, which are prevalent in districts across the country, consume vast amounts of principals' time, putting them on a treadmill of pointless activity (Fullan, 2014, p. 77). These systems, which rely on an extremely small number of scheduled observations (two to three), have been proven to show limited results in improving teaching and subsequently learning (Saphir, 1993; Marshall, 2013). Distinguishing the difference between supervision and evaluation helps to inform principal practice and can reduce the ineffectiveness of traditional teacher appraisal systems.

Supervision is the process that occurs to help people improve. Evaluation is the event that shows whether the supervision process has been successful. Supervision is formative, evaluation is summative. Supervision of staff should be happening all year, as described in Chapters 5 and 6. This work and the supporting feedback provide the basis for teacher evaluation. Because the supervision practices outlined in this book rely on short unscheduled observations some may complain that this is an unfair practice to determine teacher competency. When these processes are implemented with trust and transparency, principals can maximize opportunities to partner with teachers to avoid negative perceptions. If the principal is engaged in this work, then using this information to evaluate teachers is a much more equitable process than traditional systems because the principal is privy to the body of the teacher's work, rather than a couple of small snapshots. Feedback is an essential component of supervision practices so teachers aren't surprised by a summative discussion of their performance, because it is simply a synthesis of the information provided throughout the year. Even if a principal is in a district where the teacher appraisal system is heavily negotiated and monitored by the teachers' union, the use of frequent feedback throughout the year provides the principal with rich background knowledge and context to conduct a "formal" observation, reducing the amount of time needed to write up a summative evaluation.

Central Office Moves

Move 1: Develop a Year-Long Professional Learning Plan for Principals

The central office administrator needs to take time in the spring to articulate a clear plan for professional development for administrators. This is more than just calendaring meeting times; it includes identifying outcomes for principal development. Ann found that the best method was to look at principal learning under two major categories. The first category was called "content learning." Content learning was focused on teaching and learning issues associated with new curriculum and instructional methods/models. For example, a year prior to implementing new math standards with a focus on student-centered/problem-based mathematics, principals engaged in learning about what the math standards were and how math instruction should be structured. Process learning is focused on helping principals develop the skills needed to develop and align the processes for school improvement. An example of process learning would be teaching principals strategies for monitoring school improvement plans and how to respond to the implementation data they collect.

In addition to determining what the focus for principal learning will be, central office staff need to ensure that they have the structures and support necessary for rich learning. Principals, like teachers, are at different stages on the continuum of learning, so a one-dimensional approach to their development is also not sufficient. Large group learning should happen during monthly professional development sessions with principals from across the district. Small group support is provided for principals through cluster visits, which take no longer than one hour and consist of a small group of principals observing best practice in a predetermined classroom. Principals identify an area within the instructional model that could deepen their learning. For example, a cluster of secondary school principals may choose to visit classrooms that demonstrate inquiry-based instruction during math and science classes. Principals follow a protocol for the observation and debriefing, focusing on their own learning rather than on teacher performance. Cluster visits occur approximately four times a year. Finally, individual coaching visits occur on a regular basis for principals, as described in Chapter 5. Central office staff members discuss teaching and learning issues the principal has identified. Topics range from guidance on staff supervision to implementation issues surrounding the building improvement plan. Deliberate and thoughtful attention must be paid to building principal development. Providing high quality learning experiences is essential and cannot be done without planning ahead.

Move 2: *Plan Summer Learning Opportunities for Teachers*

Large group professional development should be used judiciously because the effect of professional development on practice and performance is inverse to the square of its distance from the classroom (Elmore, 2008). Whole group professional development should only be used at the district level during initial implementation in order to ensure that all teachers hear the same message (system coherence), aiding in developing an awareness and knowledge of district initiatives. The authors typically designated a week in the summer to provide this training. While not all teachers can attend sessions in the summer, scheduling the sessions for the same week (i.e., last week in July) over several years allows teachers to plan schedules around this event. Scheduling the training in the summer provides flexibility. For example, teachers in Ann's district who attended sessions designated as "Early Bird" in the summer were allowed to work in their classrooms during annual preservice days held prior to students starting in August. This model made large group learning more meaningful for teachers. They weren't preoccupied with getting their rooms ready and they loved having the time back in their classrooms when they needed it the most, at the start of the year.

Have to Do: Recognize Improvement

Applying relevant knowledge about effective teaching and learning practices, solving complex problems, and building relational trust are three broad capabilities that are essential to effective leadership (Robinson, 2011). These skills and dispositions are the "how" necessary for leading teaching and learning. Even though a leader may exhibit a strength in one area (e.g., solving complex problems), competency with all of these skills is necessary due to their interdependence. A good example of the interwoven nature of these skills is when leaders take time to recognize improvement. Recognizing improvement requires the leader to use their knowledge about curriculum, assessment, and effective practices to determine if these efforts are making a difference with students. Leaders need to determine if efforts are making a difference, to what degree, and if it is significant. In order to determine significance, a leader needs knowledge in pedagogy, cirriculum, and how students learn. Recognizing improvement also requires the leader to be adept in solving complex problems. Gauging improvement is based on the targets set in the school improvement plan. This plan is a result of discerning the challenges in the school and crafting solutions—the essence of problem solving. Finally, recognizing improvement models competence and integrity, two of the determinants of relational trust (Bryk & Schneider, 2002). It takes a degree of competence to determine if improvements have been made and this competence is on display when improvements are openly recognized. Integrity is about leaders keeping their word, walking the talk. In schools, integrity means that the leader's actions reaffirm the mission of the institution. Integrity is inherent when leaders share student progress publicly and recognize those who worked so diligently to make the progress happen.

Recognizing improvement is not a "nice to have" practice, but a "must have" practice for a healthy school environment. Recognizing improvement should happen all year for teachers and students, but in the spring it becomes an essential practice that helps motivate staff by reinforcing the shared sense of what is important in the school and the shared commitment to helping students learn. The key to making this an effective practice is making sure that recognition for staff is around tangible goals aligned to school improvement efforts.

Reflective Questions

Development Stage

- What improvements have we made? What data do I have to support this?
- What method(s) will I use to communicate and celebrate?

Refinement Stage

● What improvements have we made and how do they compare to progress at this time last year?

● Have the methods I have been using to communicate and celebrate progress been effective?

Principal Moves

Move 1: Celebrate Accomplishments through Reflection

The constructivist approach to learning for students encourages them to use active techniques (experiments, real-world problem solving) to create more knowledge and then to reflect on and talk about what they are doing so they can see how their understanding is changing. Having staff construct knowledge on effective teaching practices through reflection helps deepen understanding and should be an ongoing process in PLCs. Throughout the year staff must be mindful to how close their students are to 80 percent mastery on summative and formative assessments. In the spring, staff need to review a culmination of their data in order to reflect on overall effectiveness and identify changes that may need to be in place for the upcoming year. Reflective questions that must be asked of staff during the spring include:

● What generalizations or patterns do you see in your data?

● How many of your students recorded a year's growth in a year's time?

● How much growth did Tier 1 students make in comparison to students not in Tier 1?

● What evidence do you have that points to proficiency?

● Where did you see the most student growth? On what measure? How did you make that happen? What practices do you need to replicate with future students? What practices do you need to discontinue with future students?

Question 1: How familiar are you with using the school improvement strategy formative assessment?

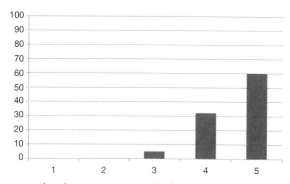

1 = unfamiliar to 5 = extremely familiar

Question 2: How familiar are you with using Hess's Matrix (action step 1)?

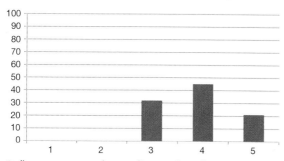

Reflect on your understanding and implementation of this step

How often do you use the proficiency statements when planning or responding to students (action step 2)?

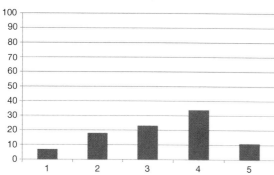

Reflect on your understanding and implementation of this action step

Figure 7.2 Staff Reflection on SIP

In addition to reflecting on student progress, staff should also be asked to reflect on the school improvement plan. For each strategy and action step within a goal area, staff rate themselves. They can then provide an example from their work that exemplifies the strategy or action step in practice. It is important to ask staff to provide examples as it helps inform the leadership team on the depth of understanding. The correlation between the Likert scale rating and the example provides rich data. For example, if on the Likert scale a teacher or team of teachers rate themselves highly on use of a practice, but when they provide a rationale for this rating based on student work the strategy is simply restated, it is clear that more teacher support is needed. This process helps staff reflect on their growth and is invaluable to the leadership team as they determine which strategies or actions need to continue and which have been accomplished. Depending on the size of the building, this can be done either in teams or individually. Figure 7.2 is an example of data collected from an end-of-year reflection.

Move 2: Plan Transitions for Students

It is imperative that clear processes and procedures are in place to transition students from one grade level to the next during the spring. Precious instructional time can be lost when student needs are discovered in the fall rather than documented and known before challenges arise. In the early spring a database with every student's name for the next year needs to be created. Included in the database are achievement, demographic, and anecdotal data. Suggestions that may help the upcoming teacher (e.g., student works better with Student X than Student Y) are also included. After staff have had adequate time to fill out the data (typically a month), meetings are scheduled with teachers and support staff (e.g., counselors and special education) who currently work with the students and those who could potentially be working with the students the next year. A structured protocol should be used—see Table 7.4—for efficiency. Identifying students who need extra assistance is necessary at this time of year so that resources can be aligned. Having intimate knowledge about behavior and academic needs of students ensures that there is a plan in place if extreme situations occur.

Table 7.4 Transition Protocol

3 – 2 – 1 **R**eport, **R**eflect, **R**ecommend Student Need Protocol
Roles: **Recorder**: Takes notes that capture group discussion **Reporter**: Delivers new information **Recipient**: Receives new information
Report (3 minutes)
Team familiar with the student (Reporters) • One team member (the Reporter) takes 3 minutes to concisely present information to the group • Include key ideas and details that will be critical to understand the student • Ask supporting members to add critical details that may have been omitted
Reflect or Clarify (2 minutes)
Team less familiar with the student (Recipients) • Whip around to ask clarifying questions • Paraphrase for understanding • Restate for clarity
Recommend for Action (1 minute)
Gather information (Recorder) • Recorder: List two to three action steps that will benefit the student • Follow up with recommendations

Central Office Move

Move: Identify District Growth through a Summative Analysis

During the spring the central office leader needs to develop a report with accompanying data that helps teachers, administrators, and board members have a greater understanding of the teaching and learning issues and student achievement measures in the district. Ann called this the State of the Schools report and used it to provide an in-depth analysis of the school district and to assist in decision-making regarding teaching and learning.

The report should contain a portfolio of data that helps the leader analyze multiple data points from different measures in order to develop conclusions about overall progress.

The central office leader must be accountable for collecting, analyzing, and making sense of the measurements that are at the heart of the district's and school's goals. While the central office leader may have support in organizing data, the leader needs to develop the analyses because an in-depth understanding of the current status of the school district is necessary to effect positive changes. The analysis is a proactive approach to identifying the work that needs to be done in the district. Developing this report will also serve as a model for building principals who will be asked to develop their own portfolio, as described in Chapter 8. By developing this report, central office administrators demonstrate to principals that they are not being asked to do something that central office administrators aren't willing to do themselves.

The contents of the report should include data that reflects progress on district goals. For example, if a district had a goal to reduce dropouts and increase graduation rates then a section would need to be devoted to that data. Each data section of the report should include an executive summary that follows the same format, to provide consistency for readers. The format that Ann used included background/rationale, data summary in the form of bullet points, conclusions and recommendations, and a list of the tables. Figure 7.3 provides an example of the table of contents for this type of report. The availability of electronic data makes this report easier to organize into an online database or portfolio. However, although technology can help with data organization and presentation, the analysis still needs to be done the old-fashioned way. The central office administrator needs to take time to draw conclusions from the data; developing executive summaries aids in this process and is a critical step not to be skipped.

Summary

During the spring a leader can begin to see the fruits of their labor if they stay committed to working school improvement processes, promoting a healthy culture, and supporting teacher development. They accomplish this by planting one foot solidly in the current school year and maintaining efforts, while the other foot is planted in planning forward. Making sure

I. District Overview

- Introduction and Overview to State of the Schools Report
- Council Bluffs Community Schools Comprehensive School Improvement Plan (CSIP)

II. Demographics

- Background and Executive Summary
- District Enrollment Trends
- Student Attendance Data
- Suspensions and Expulsions
- Free and Reduced Lunch Report
- Student Mobility Report
- Elementary Retention Report
- Elementary Class Size Report
- Equity Enrollment Data

III. AYP/APR

- adequate yearly progress (AYP)/annual progress report (APR) Background and Executive Summary
- APR Overview Report
- District AYP
- Building AYP

IV. High School Indicators of Success

- Background and Executive Summary
- ACT Longitudinal Report
- Advanced Placement Dual Credit Report
- ASSEST/COMPASS Testing
- Graduation Rates and Dropout
- Graduate Follow-Up
- PLAN

Figure 7.3 Sample Table of Contents from State of the Schools Report

V. Literacy

- Background and Executive Summary
- Iowa State Assessments
- Marie Clay
- Scholastic Reading Inventory
- Modes of Expression
- Writing on Demand
- Data Wall Reading and Writing
- Special Education/English language learner (ELL)/ talented and gifted (TAG) Achievement

VI. Mathematics

- Background and Executive Summary
- Iowa State Assessments
- Elementary Mid-Year Assessment
- Elementary End of the Year Assessment
- Data Wall
- Junior High End of Year Assessment
- High School Algebra and Geometry
- Special Education/ELL/TAG Achievement

VII. Intervention Programs

- Background and Executive Summary
- Reading Recovery
- Literacy Tier 1
- CIM Intervention
- Math Tier 1

VIII. Library Media

- Background and Executive Summary
- Collection, Circulation, and Staffing Report

IX. District Climate Survey Data

- Background and Executive Summary
- District Survey Data

Figure 7.3 continued

that learning is occurring for students and staff and recognizing improvement are actions that will help ensure continued growth for the school and the system.

Planting Seeds

In one of the many exercise phases that Ann has attempted, she tried an hour-long exercise class at a pilates studio. The emphasis here is *hour* because the instructor used every bit of that hour and then some. On average the class ended up taking 1 hour and 8 minutes. While that may not seem like a big deal, those extra minutes mattered, for the obvious reasons of course, but also because of what those minutes communicated to everyone in the class. By stretching the participants a little further each time, the instructor was telling the class that this is important work, you can't stop, you have to work hard up to the last minute. What a great way to approach the spring in schools.

Many adults in schools are ready for a break and counting down the last days, as are students. There are tons of extra chores for school staff—inventory, cleaning, packing, etc.—and there's never enough time to get it all done. It may be tempting to involve students in some of these end-of-year tasks, or to allow them down time while the adults are busy getting things done. However, take heed from what behavior specialists tell us—when the structure of the school day evaporates along with the instructional activities that teachers have worked so hard on all year, students are being set up for behavioral challenges. Consider the fact that there are a limited number of instructional days in a school year to inspire, teach, and motivate students. The last few days don't need to be wasted on busy work, and how unfair to make being successful harder for students in the waning days of the school year.

So, what can be done to avoid this trap? As a leader, model by example, don't veer from weekly walkthroughs and feedback. Continue to use PLC time to focus on student work. Be clear in expectations to staff, let them know a strong finish is sometimes what helps win the race. Generate a sense of urgency about how important every minute of every day is for students. Develop strategies that send students off with books/ideas/projects that help them support their learning throughout the summer. Use this time wisely. It is something we will never get back.

References

Aronson, J., Zimmerman, J., & Carlos, L. (1998). *Improving student achievement by extending school: Is it just a matter of time?* San Francisco, CA: WestEd.

Blai, B., Jr. (1986). Education reform: It's about "time." *Clearing House*, 60 (1), 38–40.

Bryk, A. S., & Schneider, B. L. (2002). *Trust in schools: A core resource for improvement.* New York: Russell Sage Foundation.

Elmore, R. F. (2004). *School reform from the inside out.* Cambridge, MA: Harvard Education Press.

Elmore, R. F. (2008). Leadership as the practice of improvement. In Pont, B., Nusche, D., & Hopkins, D. (Eds.), *Improving school leadership, volume 2: Case studies on system leadership* (pages 21–25), 2nd ed. Paris: Organisation for Economic Co-operation and Development.

Fullan, M. (2003). *Leadership and sustainability: System thinkers in action.* London: Sage Publishers.

Fullan, M. (2010). *All systems go: The change imperative for whole system reform.* Thousand Oaks, CA: Corwin Press & Ontario Principals' Council.

Fullan, M. (2014). *The principal: Three keys to maximizing impact.* San Francisco, CA: Jossey-Bass/Ontario Principals' Council.

Honig, M. I., Copland, M. A., Rainey, L., Lorton, J. A., & Newton, M. (2010). *Central office transformation for district-wide teaching and learning improvement.* Seattle, WA: Center for the Study of Teaching and Policy.

Joyce, B., & Showers, B. (1980). Improving inservice training: The messages of research. *Educational Leadership*, 37 (5), 379–385.

Marshall, K. (2013). *Rethinking teacher supervision and evaluation: How to work smart, build collaboration, and close the achievement gap,* 2nd ed. San Francisco, CA: Jossey-Bass.

Pont, B., & Hopkins, D. (2008). Approaches to system leadership: Lessons learned and policy pointers. In Pont, B., Nusche, D., & Hopkins, D. (Eds.), *Improving school leadership, volume 2: Case studies on system leadership* (pages 253–270), 2nd ed. Paris: Organisation for Economic Co-operation and Development.

Reeves, D. (2010). *Transforming professional development into student results.* Alexandria, VA: Association for Supervision and Curriculum Development.

Robinson, V. M. J. (2011). *Student-centered leadership.* Hoboken, NJ: Jossey-Bass.

Saphir, J. (1993). *How to make supervision and evaluation really work.* Acton, MA: Research for Better Teaching.

Summer

Reflecting, Refining, and Planning

Gardening is learning, learning, learning. That's the fun of them. You're always learning.

Helen Mirren

One of the joys of gardening is to see hard work bear fruit when the garden blooms. Even though digging, weeding, and trimming are backbreaking work, admiring the beauty of the garden makes all of the effort worthwhile. Watching and tending to a seed from planting to harvest is rewarding. Gardeners recognize this and take stock of their garden so they can replicate these efforts during the next planting season. The conditions necessary for plants to thrive are noted. When a gardener is mystified by a lack of growth they seek information that will help them understand the best conditions that nurture plant growth. They understand that digging in the dirt can actually improve a plant's performance over time. Regular tilling and mending of the soil make it easier to work with, so deliberate attention is paid to the environment. Gardeners know that if they want to continue to enjoy the fruits of their labor, they need to assess the garden and adjust practices so that the garden will continue to thrive.

Summer can also be a rewarding time for a leader and their teams if they take time to reflect on their work. Taking time to understand the conditions necessary for growth of both staff and students is an essential practice during these months. Leaders need to identify practices that resulted in improved student achievement. Identifying the environment that is most conducive to growth helps the leader know what to have in place by the fall. The "have to dos" in the summer include:

● Have to Do: Conduct a summative analysis of the data.

● Have to Do: Reflect and respond.

● Have to Do: Tend to the environment.

Have to Do: Conduct a Summative Analysis of the Data

The problem schools currently face with data is not that it doesn't exist, but rather identifying which data has relevance and what to do once the data is analyzed. One of the reasons leaders stumble with their use of data is because they get stuck on collection and organization. To use data effectively, leaders need to think of data analysis as a cycle (see Figure 8.1). Each step in this cycle has a specific purpose, and without focused attention on each phase, utilizing data for focused action becomes extremely difficult if not impossible.

Figure 8.1 The Data Analysis Cycle

Data Analysis Cycle

Data Collection

The first phase in the data analysis cycle is to collect data. While this sounds like a straightforward task, many of today's schools have sophisticated student management and learning management systems that can make this feel like an insurmountable task. In order to simplify this process, leaders must first identify available data sources. Leadership teams need to brainstorm a list of all of the demographic, perceptual, school process, and student learning data in their building and how often it is collected (Bernhardt, 2002). While analyzing high stakes tests (i.e., state assessments that determine Every Child Achieves status) is a part of the puzzle, high achieving schools understand that other measures of student learning need to be collected such as running records, unit assessments, etc. A common list of questions that will help facilitate the brainstorming process as it pertains to student achievement data is found in Table 8.1 (Mooney & Mausbach, 2008).

After the identification of existing data the next step is to select which data points will help answer critical questions. A focused way to accomplish this with a team is to complete the organizer found in Table 8.2. As the team works through this organizer they have to keep this question in mind, "Is this data just interesting or is the data really important in helping us answer questions or identify next steps?" This approach avoids the time-consuming process of analyzing every piece of data just because it exists

Table 8.1 Brainstorming Questions for Collection of Achievement Data

- What type of information do you collect on a regular basis (quarter, semester, trimester)?
- What evidence is available to help understand various levels of student achievement? For secondary teachers is this collected by content area?
- What district-wide classroom assessments are administered in your school?
- What intervention data is collected, specifically classroom interventions (Tier 1)?

Table 8.2 Determining Importance Data Form

FOCUS AREA	QUESTIONS NEEDING ANSWERED	DATA POINTS
Demographics *(enrollment, attendance, dropout, ethnicity, gender)*		
Perception *(student, parent, staff surveys, social media comments, parent involvement numbers)*		
School Improvement Processes *(evidence of attainment of SIP strategies, walkthrough data, implementation studies)*		
Student Learning *(state assessments, district assessments, teacher-created common assessments, teacher observations)*		

EXAMPLE

FOCUS AREA	QUESTIONS NEEDING ANSWERED	DATA POINTS
Demographics *(enrollment, attendance, dropout, ethnicity, gender)*	Has our student population changed over time? Do we have a mobility issue?	Longitudinal data for percent of students on free and reduced lunch, percent of ethnic groups enrolled over time. Mobility rates over time
Perception *(student, parent, staff surveys, social media comments, parent involvement numbers)*	How can we engage students in the school culture?	Enrollment in extracurricular activities over time, student perception survey data, minutes from principal round-table discussions
School Improvement Processes *(evidence of attainment of SIP strategies, walkthrough data, implementation studies)*	Did we meet the goals in our school improvement plan? Which strategies made the biggest difference in terms of student achievement? Were all strategies in the plan implemented at high levels?	State assessment achievement; percent proficient Common formative assessment data and district assessments Walkthrough feedback, implementation studies results
Student Learning *(state assessments, district assessments, teacher-created common assessments, teacher observations)*	Are all of our students growing at the expected rate? Are we closing achievement gap? Are interventions making a difference? Is there one Tier that is not having desired impact?	State assessments: Comparison of student growth versus expected growth for all students and subgroups Progress monitoring data over time for Tier 1, Tier 2, and Tier 3

	Grades	Number of Students Served	Number of Students Exiting by Growth	Percentage of Students Exiting by Growth
Reading Intervention I				
2009–10	7–8th	45	15	33%
2010–11	7th			
	8th	18		
	7–8th			
2011–12	7th	47		
	8th	36		
	7–8th	83		
Reading Intervention II				
2009–10	7–8th	48	10	21%
2010–11	7th			
	8th			
	7–8th			
2011–12	7th	33		
	8th	26		
	7–8th	59		
Cumulative Totals				
2009–10	7–8th	93	25	27%
2010–11	7–8th			
2011–12	7–8th	142		

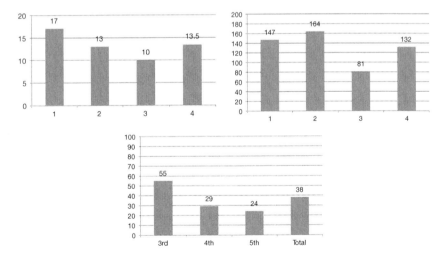

Figure 8.2 Data Presentation Examples

and wasting one of the most critical commodities in an administrator's life—time.

Data Organization/Presentation

There are two basic principles that leaders need to keep in mind when organizing data: presentation matters and don't be fooled by aesthetics. In order to make sense of data, it must be organized so that trends can be identified and conclusions drawn by a broad audience. Engaging staff in understanding school data is essential for whole school reforms. When data is confusing or disorganized it leads to frustration and at its worst may cause a school to adopt an initiative that won't meet the needs of students. Figure 8.2 illustrates the importance of presenting data in a coherent way. Both samples are looking at intervention data; sample A is difficult to read and analyze, while conclusions can easily be drawn from sample B.

Using printouts from the school's data warehouse or charts provided by central office may be useful, and the authors are proponents of not recreating the wheel; however, many times the way the data is presented isn't organized in a manner that helps develop understanding. Relying solely on these printouts limits the depth of analysis. Principals need to be able to create their own charts and graphs organized in a way that lends itself to interpretation.

The purpose of putting numbers in a chart or graph is to communicate the data in a clear and concise manner. It is easy to get caught up in making a chart that is aesthetically pleasing, but doesn't help answer the critical questions in the school. In Figure 8.3 graduation data is presented. While sample A is aesthetically pleasing, making conclusions based on that data is limited. Sample B, however, a simple chart, includes information that would allow a data team to draw several conclusions.

Data Analysis

Once relevant data has been collected and organized, data analysis can begin. This is not to suggest that data analysis shouldn't be happening throughout the year. It absolutely should be happening during weekly PLCs. However, the summer months provide an opportunity for principals to get

Sample A: Original Year of Graduation

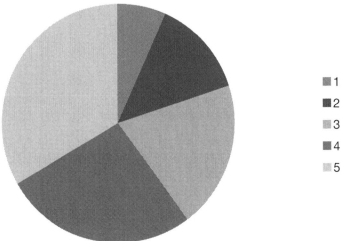

Sample B

Student original graduation year	Total number of students	Percentage	Special Education	Percentage of Special Education
2013	7	8.4%	1	6.25%
2012	36	43.4%	7	43.75%
2011	28	33.7%	6	37.5%
2010	7	8.4%	1	6.25%
2009	5	6%	1	6.25%

*Figure 8.*3 Data Aesthetics

a comprehensive summative look at all of the building data. Principals need to develop a data portfolio that includes analysis and action. The process of developing this portfolio and participating in a data consult leads directly to the school improvement plan. Without conducting this in-depth analysis of all the building's data the school runs the risk of developing a plan that doesn't address the central needs of the school. Once the data portfolio is developed, the principal needs to participate in a data consult. Both processes are critical if a school is going to take responsibility for the data, which are discussed in the "Moves" sections of the chapter.

Data Accountability

Data accountability occurs through alignment of the blueprint processes. The data portfolio and data consult are used to identify school improvement needs. A plan is developed to address needs and through the use of walkthroughs and look fors the plan is monitored. When there is a direct connection to each of the processes, data accountability is inevitable. The key is making sure there is strong alignment. Refer back to Figure 8.1 to see how accountability fits into the cycle.

Data Engagement

All of this work will be for naught if the principal doesn't engage staff in both analysis and understanding of what the data is communicating, and identifying actions to address needs. There is no one right way to engage staff in the process, but typically there are two methods principals use.

Method One: After Portfolio & Consult. Principals may develop the portfolio without a lot of upfront input from staff and engage staff after the portfolio and consult, many times during fall preservice days. After engaging the entire staff in a review of data, principals ask teachers to develop big ideas and actions the building needs to take. Building leadership teams uses these ideas as the plan is developed. After the large group analysis takes place, teachers may be asked to develop a mini portfolio on their individual achievement data and meet with the principal in what we refer to as a mini consult. These conversations lead to development of the teacher's individual professional development plan for the year. Principals who are new to the building typically use this method.

Method Two: Before Portfolio & Consult. Many principals have staff help them develop the portfolio and engage staff in identifying just the facts, big ideas, and action steps. This collective work becomes a part of the portfolio. This provides shared ownership and makes the development of the portfolio a less daunting task for building leadership. This process typically starts with large group analysis and then moves to working teams around the sections of the portfolio. If state assessment data is not available until late in the school year the level of participation of staff needs to be considered, as this typically occurs in the extremely busy month of May.

Reflective Questions

Development Stage

- What sources of data are currently easily accessible?
- What are the most crucial data points that need to be analyzed? Do these align with the mission, vision, and beliefs?
- How will staff be engaged in this process?

Refinement Stage

- Which part of the data analysis cycle needs more attention?
- Are there new or different data points that need to be considered?
- Did the methods for engaging staff in data analysis have the desired results?
- Do any adjustments need to be made to schedules in order to ensure that supervision practices are conducted on an ongoing basis?

Principal Move

Move: Analyze Data, Develop a Portfolio, and Participate in a Data Consult

The data portfolio is a tool the principal uses in order to help make decisions about the next steps in the school's improvement journey. Guiding questions developed in collaboration with central office staff help principals focus on all aspects of the school. Principals are encouraged to chunk their data into meaningful parts. Typical sections in a portfolio include demographics, literacy (including intervention data), mathematics (including intervention data), and culture and climate. The purpose of the data portfolio is to help the building principal synthesize multiple data points so that appropriate decisions and actions can be made that will address the school's needs. Principals are trained to use a three-step process to facilitate interpretation. The three steps listed below should be developed for each section of the school portfolio.

Step One: Just the Facts. The first step in analyzing the data is to act like Joe Friday from *Dragnet* and stick to the facts. Principals are asked to review the data and identify facts in a clear and concise way. Essential questions help to filter and shift out the important data and provide relevance to data collection. The process of answering the essential questions focuses on relevant data points so "facts" that matter can be identified. Examples of effective questions follow.

● How effective was the school improvement plan?

Data points include: implementation data, impact (achievement) data including formative and summative data

● What environmental factors influenced achievement?

Data points include: surveys, discipline, demographics

● Did the school meet Adequate Yearly Progress (AYP)?

Data points include: state assessments including subgroups

● What effect has differentiated instruction had on student achievement?

Data points include: achievement for special populations, Special Education, English Language Learners, at-risk, talented and gifted

An inquiry process is used to help answer essential questions. Figure 8.4 provides an example of the questions used to help arrive at the facts. In order to avoid a long list of facts that may prohibit analysis, principals are trained to develop the facts as follows.

● Summarize information from data sources into a bullet point.

o *Example:* 76 percent of students in 3rd grade scored at the proficient level in mathematics on state assessments.

● Combine and summarize facts to show a trend or pattern.

o *Example:* Scores for 7th graders increased in the intermediate and high bands for both science and math compared to the previous year.

● Restate the facts by using other statistical measures to simplify and clarify the data.

o *Example:* The percent of 11th graders who scored below proficient was reduced by half from the previous year.

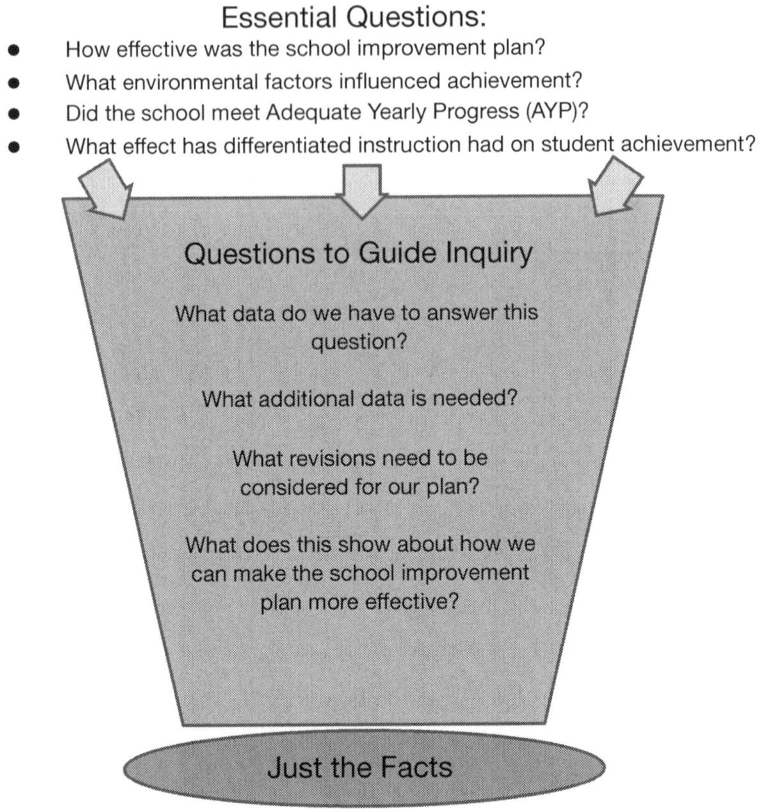

Essential Questions:

- How effective was the school improvement plan?
- What environmental factors influenced achievement?
- Did the school meet Adequate Yearly Progress (AYP)?
- What effect has differentiated instruction had on student achievement?

Questions to Guide Inquiry

What data do we have to answer this question?

What additional data is needed?

What revisions need to be considered for our plan?

What does this show about how we can make the school improvement plan more effective?

Just the Facts

Figure 8.4 Inquiry Process for Developing Just the Facts

Step Two: Big Ideas. Big ideas are summary statements derived from "just the facts" to provide insight into what the data means. Big ideas answer the "so what" question. So what does all the data mean? Big ideas should be similar to the findings in a professional research study as they serve as the conclusion based on the facts. Many times big ideas can lead principals and central office staff to the conclusion that more data is needed to confirm or test a hypothesis. Following are examples of big ideas:

- A school-wide student support system developed this year has resulted in improvements in office referrals; however, work needs to continue in this area with a focus on including teachers in the process so it is more efficient for students.

● Kindergarten data indicates that students' scores are improving throughout the year as compared to previous years. However, achievement of students at first and second grade has dropped or been stagnant. A review of interventions and supports in the early grades needs to occur.

Step Three: Action. After big ideas have been generated, principals need to identify actions that address issues that surfaced during the analysis. Principals are encouraged to identify "big wheel" and "little wheel" actions. Big wheel actions are those that will take a significant amount of time and effort to implement. These actions must be connected back to the school's overall improvement plan. "Little wheel" actions are those items that just need to get done and more than likely will not end up in the school improvement plan. An example of a big wheel action is shared below aligned to big ideas. An example of a little wheel action would be something like, "Update school posters to reflect change in procedures." Table 8.3 provides an example of aligned big ideas and action steps.

Table 8.3 Big Ideas Aligned to Action Steps

BIG IDEAS:
• Tier 1 interventions are closing the gap and moving students within bands on the data wall.
• Shared instructional focus between classroom and intervention teachers has had a strong impact on student achievement.
• Expected growth gains on state assessment are due to the focus on teaching the curriculum and increasing the amount of reading volume for all students.
ACTION STEPS:
• Continue to build shared meaning on Common Core through vertical study.
• Plan, implement, and support K-1 teachers with literacy stations in order to continue to increase reading volume.
• Continue to work in learning teams to create and implement Tier 1 interventions based on common formative assessments.

When developing action steps, principals need to keep five factors in mind (Mooney & Mausbach, 2008):

1. **Target individual students.** Use data to identify action for those students who are not making expected growth.

2. **Align curriculum to standards.** If assessments are aligned to standards, use data to pinpoint deficits in specific curriculum strands.

3. **Ensure full implementation of best practices.** Use data to determine the level of implementation of best practices targeted as essential for improved achievement. Leaders need to consider the level of implementation before adding or abandoning new practices.

4. **Align classroom instruction to assessment.** Use data to pinpoint specific assessment methods that need to be addressed in the classroom.

5. **Identify personnel concerns.** Use data to identify teachers who consistently help students to excel in order to encourage them to share knowledge and expertise. If a teacher has a pattern of low achievement, data coupled with an appropriate evaluation process can be used to help improve teacher performance.

Armed with the school portfolio and a rough draft of the school improvement plan, the building principal is ready for the data consult. The data consult is a chance for the building principal to talk out loud about the needs of their school with an active listener. Having the opportunity to problem-solve with a "knowledgeable other" on issues directly related to their school's context increases the principal's confidence in the course charted for the school.

Central Office Moves

Move 1: Provide Guiding Questions for Development of the Data Portfolio

In order to provide principals with the support they need to develop a data portfolio, central office administrators need to develop guiding questions that will help principals navigate the analysis process. These guiding questions are developed in collaboration with building principals and serve as a *framework* for analysis. The questions aren't meant to be used as an exhaustive checklist that the building principal must plod through. These questions are designed to help the principal look at all facets of the school using all the data available within the district/school. An example of guiding questions generated by central office administration can be found in Appendix G. Central office should encourage principals to use this as a guide as they work through the process described in the previous principal move.

Move 2: Conduct Data Consults

The data consult is a powerful conversation about the teaching and learning needs in the school. The data consult is a 90-minute meeting with a central office administrator to discuss the summary statements from the school portfolio. A major purpose of the data consult is to help make decisions about the next steps in the school improvement and professional development plan. The meeting begins with the building principal providing a summary of what is in the data portfolio specifically around big ideas. Once the data is shared, the remainder of the meeting is dedicated to what actions the principal is considering as a result of the analysis and how this will impact the school improvement plan.

The data consults provide the central office administrator with a wealth of information that guides decision-making. The power in these one-on-one conversations is that it provides an opportunity for the central office leader to develop deeper understanding of issues that may have surfaced throughout the year. Data consults provide an upfront look at the issues of teaching and learning and allow the central office administrator to note patterns across schools. Information discussed helps the central office administrator confirm or deny hypotheses and define next steps in both the area of curriculum and principal development. Consults offer another layer of support and provide opportunities for discrete coaching with a principal.

Central office administrators have to provide explicit training on developing the portfolio and expectations of the data consult in order to ensure that principals follow the data analysis cycle and do not spin their wheels collecting and analyzing data that is interesting, but doesn't impact school outcomes. Table 8.4 provides an overview of the roles and responsibilities for both the data portfolio and consult.

Table 8.4 Roles and Responsibilities for Data Consult and Portfolio

Tool	Central Office Administrator's Role	Building Principal's Role
Data Portfolio	• Provide guiding questions • Make sure data is easily accessible • Train principals on the data analysis cycle process	• Collect and organize data • Develop a portfolio that contains facts, big ideas, and action steps
Data Consult	• Complete an individual school analysis form • Identify questions that need to be addressed during the consult • Schedule and organize consults	• Review data in portfolio • Identify important points that need to be shared • Include an overview of tentative school improvement plan

Have to Do: Reflect and Respond

As important as data analysis is to decision-making, it can't be the sole determiner. This may sound ironic after reading the previous section, but in addition to good data leaders need to make decisions based on previous practice. Using lessons learned from doing the work helps the leader make stronger judgments. Effective decision-making requires equal measures of data and experience. In order to learn from practice, leaders need to process experiences using reflection.

Reflective practice involves three types of reflection: reflection in action, on action, and about the action (Schon, 1987; Fullan & Hargreaves, 2012). Reflection in and on action, as previously described in Chapter 6, is the ability to solve a problem while in the middle of it (in action) and to reflect when the practice is finished (on action). Reflection about the action is reflection about things in the environment that stand in the way of doing the important work. All three types of reflection are important as they help the leader think about not only what they did (on and in), but how they did it (about). Reflecting on the behaviors that keep the focus on the important aspects of the work improves practice because it provides the context and conditions for success. Once a leader identifies the factors in the environment that distract them from leading teaching and learning, they can make positive changes. Tracking how principals spend their time, which has come in vogue with initiatives such as the National School Administrative Manager (SAM) Innovation Project (Wallace Foundation, 2015), is designed to facilitate reflection about action so leaders spend more time on teaching and learning issues. Summer is the optimal time to engage in reflection on and about action. The months or weeks when students are not in school provide a golden opportunity for leaders to take a deep breath and think deeply about successes and misses without the ongoing distractions that are inherent when school is in session. This time for reflection helps to shape future actions and promotes the likelihood that these actions will be successful in moving the system forward.

Principal Move

Move: Read and Think

Fullan (2014, p. 98) implores leaders to "look out to improve within." Fullan uses this terminology to promote the idea that leaders in high performing systems, particularly principals, build external networks and partnerships (both within and outside the district) in order to improve. Active participation in networks helps the leader identify new ideas or practices that may be successful in the context of their school. A network is a group or system of interconnected people or things, thus implying reciprocal relationships. In strong networks leaders both learn from others and share their successes. Effective leaders know that a stronger network will be formed when they can share their learning. This requires a principal to take charge of their professional growth. During the summer, principals need to identify areas where further study is needed and read books, blogs, and articles that help deepen knowledge. For example, a high school principal whose previous experience may have been as a school counselor and science teacher understands that reading and writing across the curriculum is needed in the school, so the summer months are spent reading about effective literacy practices at the secondary level. An elementary principal who has only taught in the upper grades may find the need to understand

169

more about effective practices in the primary grades, so a study of effective practices in early childhood is warranted. The key for leaders during these months is to target an area where they know they need more background knowledge and spend time delving into learning.

Reflection during the summer must focus on how to build professional capital so teachers can continue to work together in meaningful ways. The leader needs to wrestle with the explicit actions teachers will take to impact achievement. The key to generating widespread impact on learning and culture lies in mobilizing the group to work in specific ways (Fullan, 2014). Principals need to ask questions of themselves such as, "How am I going to make processes better?", "How do I make teachers more efficient?", "How do I develop ownership for learning?", "How do I continue to empower teachers?" Kim used a survey titled "If the Principal Only Knew" at the end of the year to aid in her reflection. Questions posed provided personal information, information about the staff's role in the mission, their contribution to student achievement, and issues of concern. These types of reflection help the principal hone decisional capital in order to influence human capital throughout the school.

Central Office Move

 ### Move: Review and Revise District Curriculum

Having a guaranteed and viable curriculum is a critical factor in high performing schools (Marzano, 2003). Developing a coherent curriculum takes time and thought. This work can't be done in a vacuum; it requires the work of vertical teams from across the system. Teams need extended periods of time to concentrate on creating a well-articulated curriculum that is useful and usable for teachers. Meeting once a month throughout the year isn't adequate because it doesn't allow for continuity of thought and causes a lot of false starts and stops as educators try to decipher where they left off from the previous meeting. Curriculum revision should happen in the summer months when teachers can give this work their undivided attention. The cost for setting aside this time may be a barrier for districts large and small. However, a strong curriculum has been proven to make a difference in teaching and learning. Writing curriculum and ensuring its implementation warrants top priority in the budget.

Ann implemented a process called Curriculum Camp that was held every summer. Curriculum Camp is a designated week where teachers spend consecutive days, typically a week, developing curriculum and assessments without interruptions. Typically two Curriculum Camps were held each summer. A five-day camp was scheduled for the curriculum that was under major revision. A mini camp, two to three days, was held for the curriculum implemented the previous year. This is necessary because despite teams' best efforts, after one year of implementation there are always some assessments and pacing issues that need to be adjusted. Camps are scheduled in early June prior to summer school so teachers are available, allowing central office staff the months of June and July to ensure that the curriculum documents developed are in order and ready to distribute in the fall.

With the advent of the Common Core Curriculum Standards many districts may feel that time developing district-wide curriculum is no longer necessary. Leaders need to remember that the Common Core is a set of standards and as such districts need to spend time helping to make sense of the standards by developing curriculum documents and assessments that promote high levels of understanding and implementation. The Common Core standards help with efficiency of curriculum development because teams no longer need to spend time haggling over what content belongs where, but time still needs to be spent on unpacking and understanding what these standards are asking of our students.

Have to Do: Tend to the Environment

Chapter 3 outlined how vital a healthy culture is to high performing systems. Healthy student-centered cultures, according to Peterson and Deal (1998), are places where the underlying norms are collegiality, improvement, and hard work. Rituals and traditions celebrate not only student accomplishments, but teacher innovation and parental commitment. These norms are fostered in a hospitable to learning environment. A hospitable to learning environment is one that is friendly toward new ideas and welcoming to those who struggle to question themselves and their learning (Toll, 2010). In this type of environment, teachers do not have to hide what they know and don't know; and parents feel welcomed when they come to the school. This means more than providing treats at meetings and having lamps and plants in the office. In essence a hospitable school provides comfortable spaces in which to do uncomfortable work. When difficult examinations of past-held beliefs or current failed efforts take place these struggles can occur within a culture that can honor that work and move on to new learning. For this to happen the principal must conscientiously create spaces in the school both in and outside of classrooms that welcome learning. During the summer months leaders need to take stock of their surroundings and ask themselves, "Is this space conducive to learning?"

Principal Move

Move: Create an Invitational Setting

The environment in schools speaks volumes about the values in a school. Chapter 6 discussed the message that is being sent when the walls of a school are bare versus walls that display student learning. In an open learning environment, principals understand that the climate of the school is shaped by the decisions they make, large and small, about environment. For example, Kim changed from using bells to signal class changes to using music. This simple but subtle change helped to create an entirely different mood during passing periods.

During the summer months principals must make sure to create or update the spaces that invite learning. These spaces are found in the common areas of the school as well as in classrooms. First impressions are powerful and lasting. Thus, tending to the aesthetics of the front entrance and foyer of the school is imperative. When the principal tends to the physical environment in the summer, teachers return in the fall and are inspired to do the same in their classrooms.

Central Office Move

Move: Provide Resources Necessary for Safe and Inviting Settings

Central office administrators need to partner with facilities and maintenance staff to make sure that furnishings for schools support the teaching and learning objectives of the system. How money is spent on learning spaces sends a strong message on the values of the organization. Purchasing tables rather than desks communicates the importance of collaboration. Developing classroom furniture standards K-12 that include soft seating demonstrates a commitment to movement and promoting stress-free learning environments. Decisions made about the physical assets of the school should align with the organization's mission and vision. The summer months should be used to take inventory of the current status and devote resources to making sure schools have what they need to create safe and invitational learning environments.

Summary

During the summer months the commitments to school improvement, a healthy culture, and development of professional capital are evident when leaders tend to data analysis, spend time on reflection, and organize learning environments. Attention to these important tasks during the summer months sets up the school for the important work that needs to happen during the fall.

Planting a Seed: What the Nike FuelBand Teaches Us About Leadership

Ann was so excited to get a Nike FuelBand; that was until she found out how sedentary her life was. The cool thing about the Nike band is that besides tracking steps, it reminds you once an hour to get up and move for 5 minutes. Every time you do this you get a point and "win" the hour. It also tracks what it calls fuel points. Fuel points are basically an indication of how much energy you exert in a given day.

Suffice it to say the first couple of weeks tracking this data were rough for Ann. She rarely hit her daily goal for fuel points and was lucky to "win" one hour a day. The numbers bewildered her. She had always prided herself on being very active. She parked her car in the far end of parking lots, she took the stairs to her office rather than use the elevator, and she exercised for 30 minutes at least three times a week. What she found out is that these things are not enough. How could this be?

After digging into the data she realized a few things. While she was going to the gym she really wasn't exerting too much energy. Her 30 minutes on the elliptical were not as intense as when she walked/ran on the treadmill. She also realized that if she spent 45 minutes exercising rather than 30, the benefits were significant. Finally, a regular reminder to get moving makes a difference. So after making changes to her exercise routine and moving more throughout the day, her data started to improve. She is so grateful for this tool because without it she would have had no idea of the level of her inactivity. She had been wondering why she wasn't seeing results on the scales and now she had some concrete evidence as to why, and, more importantly, could take some action to correct this.

As leaders of improvement efforts in schools there is a lot we can learn from Ann's Nike FuelBand experience.

- We have all heard the saying that the definition of crazy is doing the same thing and expecting different results. This happens, not because we are crazy, but because we can't define the problem. We can't define the problem because we aren't collecting the right data. Up until the FuelBand Ann's only measure of progress was the scales. While this is an important measure, it isn't diagnostic in nature, it is a summative measure. So too are the high stake assessments or standardized achievement tests in schools. This information simply doesn't give a leader enough information to clearly identify and define issues with achievement.

- Consistent monitoring of things that matter makes a difference. School improvement plans have a bad rap because of this very issue. Seldom are the measures of success clearly identified or monitored. Leaders monitor by having a clear set of look fors and conducting walkthroughs, general and focused, and implementation studies on a regular basis (not just once a year) to determine levels of implementation. The ability to have a common measure (fuel points) allowed Ann to see patterns and trends in her exercise regimen. When principals monitor with a common measure (look fors) they get a clearer picture of what is happening or not happening in the school.

- The key to improvement isn't the tool, but what we do with it. Ann is certain she would have never figured out her level of inactivity without the band; however, those scales won't move unless she uses the information from the band to change behaviors. Principals need tools as well—a school improvement and professional development plan, data consults, etc.—but if principals don't use the tools to help them inform their practice, they are meaningless.

● Being relentless, in fitness or leadership, is critical to success. As much as Ann wishes she could only exercise two or three days a week and expect changes she knows that at her age that won't cut it. School leaders have to be relentless in pursuit of their school improvement efforts. They need to be continually looking for evidence of implementation and making sense of what they see in classrooms and student work.

It's time to get moving. Just do it!

References

Bernhardt, V. (2002). *The school portfolio toolkit*. Larchmont, NY: Eye on Education.

Fullan, M. (2014). *The principal: Three keys to maximizing impact*. San Francisco, CA: Jossey-Bass.

Fullan, M., & Hargreaves, A. (2012). *Professional capital: Transforming teaching in every school*. New York: Teachers College Press.

Marzano, R. J. (2003). *What works in schools: Translating research into actions*. Alexandria, VA: Association for Supervision of Curriculum and Development.

Mooney, N., & Mausbach, A. (2008). *Align the design: A blueprint for school improvement*. Alexandria, VA: Association for Supervision of Curriculum and Development.

Peterson, K., & Deal, T. (2009). *Shaping school culture: Pitfalls, paradoxes, and promises*. San Francisco, CA: Jossey-Bass.

Schon, D. A. (1987). *Educating the reflective practitioner: A new design for teaching and learning in the professions*. San Francisco, CA: Jossey-Bass.

Toll, C. (2010, June). Six steps to learning leadership. *Journal of Staff Development, 31* (3), 50–52, 54, 56.

Wallace Foundation (2015). The National SAM Innovation Project: Helping principals make time to focus on instructional leadership. www.wallace foundation.org/Pages/Sam.aspx

Collaborative Learning Team Agenda

Core PLC Week ___

Tuesday–Thursday–Friday

Sample Team Norms:

- We will start the meeting on time and end at the proposed time.

- We will allow others to finish thoughts before responding and be respectful with our laptops/electronics.

- Meetings should be closed to those individuals that the topic pertains to. Topics should be discussed in confidence and done as a whole group rather than small groups.

- We will be open-minded and flexible. We may not reach consensus but agree to do what works best for each of us within the agreed upon ideas. We will think about what is best for the children.

- We will honor all participants' opinions/thoughts/comments without passing judgment. We will attend all meetings; if we are unable, we will seek information missed.

- We will respect each other's points of view and be active participants in the group.

	Guiding Questions	Activities/Resources	"I Can" Reflections
Warm-up (Celebrations)	*What is our fundamental purpose and what do we value? How do we know?*		
Tuesday Phase I Content Planning Learning Team Learning/Planning What do we want all students to learn—by grade/course/unit?	What does your formative/summative assessment tell you about what students learned? What do the Phases really mean?		Notes/Group Reflection
Debrief Check for understanding	What have you accomplished during this PLC to respond to student achievement?		
Warm-up (Celebrations)	*What is our fundamental purpose and what do we value? How do we know?*		
Thursday Phase II Student Work/Assessment Learning Team Tuning Protocol	What does your formative/summative assessment tell you about what students learned?	Look at Data Data	

Formative Assessments Analysis of Student Work How will we know when each student has acquired the intended knowledge and skills?		
Warm-up (Celebrations)	*What is our fundamental purpose and what do we value? How do we know?*	
Friday *Phase III* *Content Planning* *Planning for Guided Instruction* *Tier I* *Response* How will we respond when students experience initial difficulty so that we can improve upon current levels of learning?	How can Close Reading assist non-proficient students?	Close Reading and Text Dependency: What does it mean for students who are not proficient?
Debrief Check for understanding	Reflecting on the day what questions do you have?	Q&A with discussion

APPENDIX

B

Backward Planner Template

SMART Goals (Destination)

Proficiency Statements (Vehicle)

INDICATORS "I Can" statements	Context	Advanced	Proficient	Basic	Below Basic
Curriculum or grade level expectation					

Essential Mini Lessons ("I Can")	Anchor Charts	Possible Prompts	Formative Assessments	Resources

181

Core Proficiencies

	Teacher 1	Teacher 2	Teacher 3	Teacher 4
Beginning of Year				
Benchmark One				
Benchmark Two				
Benchmark Three				
End of Year				

Tier I Target Student Proficiencies (10)

	Teacher 1	Teacher 2	Teacher 3	Teacher 4
Beginning of Year				
Benchmark One				
Benchmark Two				
Benchmark Three				
End of Year				

Scope and Sequence

	Monday	Tuesday	Wednesday	Thursday	Friday
Week 1					
Week 2					
Week 3					
Week 4					
Week 5					
Week 6					

SIP Template

Long Version

Building Name
School Improvement Plan—Part A
OVERVIEW
Updated for school year: _____

	09–10	10–11	11–12	12–13	13–14
Sept. Enrollment:					
% Free and Reduced Lunch					

School improvement team members:

Describe the primary focus of the school improvement efforts for the upcoming year.

Briefly describe the process used to update the school improvement plan.

No.	SIP Goal	Alignment to State Performance Plan – Special Education Outcomes	Alignment to District Strategic Plan/CSIP Goals
I			
II			
III			
IV			

Building Name School Improvement Plan Goals and Strategies—Part B & C
District Long Range Goal *(insert corresponding district goal):*
Diagnostic Data: *(list five years' ITBS/ITED data by grade level)*
Building Goal I:
Rationale: *(list three years' current district data that supports need for this goal)*

No.	School Strategies	Narrative Evaluation of Strategy (How will you know if strategy is working to accomplish goal?)
IA		
IB		
IC		

Monitoring Log

Goal I:	
Strategy # & Description:	

Action Steps #	Action Steps to Implement Strategy:	Person Responsible	I	P	M	C

KEY: I = Initiate, P = Progressing, M = Met, C = Canceled

Building Name School Improvement Plan Professional Development Plan—Part D	
PD Activities to Accomplish Strategies and Action Steps	
School Strategies that require Professional Development:	
No.	**Strategy**

Date	Strategy No.	Name of Activity	Description	Budget Projection and Funding Source	PD Implementation Evaluation

SIP One-Pager

Your School Name/ School Logo	Enrollment
	Free and Reduced Lunch Percentage

DATA

Reading:
Math:
Safe Schools:

STRATEGY

Reading:
Math:
Safe Schools:

EVIDENCE

FUTURE

SIP Feedback

School Improvement Plan Feedback
School Year: 2013–2014

Building: _____ Principal: _____

OVERVIEW	
Proficiency Statement	The overview section identifies the overall focus of the plan for the year. Demographic data is complete and accurate. A description of the leadership structure is included that outlines how all staff members had an opportunity for input in the development of the plan. A description of the process that will be used to update the plan is complete. All goals are listed and are aligned to the Iowa State Performance Plan Special Education Outcomes.
Feedback	• The overview helps provide a good picture of how you plan to focus your professional development so you have balance. • From the overview it appears as if you have two major foci: studying grade level expectation and formative assessment. See feedback below, but this may not be as clear or where you will end up given some of the strategies and action steps.

GOALS	
Proficiency Statement	Goals must align with the district long-range goals. Goals provide a short-term target to help meet district long-range goals. Goals match needs identified from school's data analysis. Goals include the behavior that needs to be changed, the conditions, and criteria for knowing when the goal is met. There should be no more than three goals; two should address achievement and one addresses safe schools.
Feedback	• Focusing your goals on improvement is to be commended; this is a goal that will help staff keep the focus on working with all students so growth occurs. • Decreasing the gap on the data wall is another appropriate goal; you may want to quantify that, by how much will you decrease the gap. Quantifying this will help staff know if you meet this goal. • Math and safe and respectful school goals clear and measurable.

STRATEGIES	
Proficiency Statement	Strategies identify the innovations that will help accomplish goals. One or more strategy for each goal should be identified. Strategies selected reflect best practices and current district instructional philosophy. Strategies listed are "high leverage" (likely result in goal being met). A description of how the strategy will be evaluated for effectiveness is measurable and will help determine whether strategies are working.
Feedback	• Literacy Strategy A is clear—you are working on implementing writing and reading conferences. • In your overview you state that formative assessment is the focus, but that is unclear from the way your literacy strategies are written. If you want the strategy to be the use of formative assessments (which is a good idea) then the phases and products of the learning team process can be action steps—"I Can" statements, proficiency statements, etc. Try to write this strategy as straightforward as you did Strategy A. • Strategy A in math is really around questioning correct? If so say that simply. Strategies are meant to help focus your work, as written it appears as if you are going after many aspects of math workshop—questioning, student

	reasoning, and conversational moves. It will be difficult to get good at all three all at once. • Same feedback from bullet 2 applies to your Math Strategy B. • The strategy for Goal 3 needs to be more specific. Is there a certain aspect around the Differentiated Student Support Process that you want to focus on improving this year?

ACTION STEPS	
Proficiency Statement	Action steps mean action. Action steps list the things that need to occur in order to ensure that the strategies get done. There should be a series of action steps for each strategy. Action steps identify the person or groups of people that will be primarily responsible for making sure the action step gets completed.
Feedback	• Action steps for literacy align well with Strategy A, but because Strategy B needs reworked a bit I am not sure you have a good outline here of the steps you need to accomplish to get formative assessment measures in place. • Action steps for math are fairly generic, but this may be due to the fact that both strategies need to be clarified. Take for example the second action step—set up a safe and risk taking environment—how do you plan to do this? Do staff need training; what does this look like? It is difficult to get action steps to a meaningful level (a work plan in essence) if strategies aren't clear, which I think may be the case here. • Because the strategy for Goal 3 is so generic many of the action steps are as well. The first action step is very unclear under this goal and does not help identify the work. Action steps are the "to do" part of your plan. As currently written the action steps appear to be generic and won't necessarily result in meeting your goal of attendance.

PROFESSIONAL DEVELOPMENT	
Proficiency Statement	Professional development activities are listed and align directly to strategies. Projected dates for activities are included. Evaluations of each professional development are included. Professional development activities reflect best practices in professional development.
Feedback	• Your PD plan does a good job of forecasting what you plan to do all year. • Best practice to celebrate successes mid-year. Writing this into your plan ensures you will do this. • I would carefully review what you have outlined here and ask yourself if this work is directly tied to your strategies once you rework them. You want tight alignment between the strategies, action steps, and PD.

NEXT STEPS:

1. Revisit Strategy B in literacy and both A and B in math in order to make sure that there is one clear strategy in place. Once you get those clarified you will want to look at action steps to identify which can stay, what needs added and which need deleted.

2. Identify a specific strategy or strategies for Goal 3 and develop action steps to ensure goal is accomplished.

APPENDIX

Feedback Examples from Monitoring SIP

General Walkthrough Feedback

Teachers,

Friday morning I visited several classrooms. We looked for student engagement in activities that involve higher-level learning. The purpose of this letter is to provide summative school-wide feedback to you for your reflection.

We enjoyed being in classrooms. First, we saw students doing work that was purposeful and rich. Students were able to share with us the concepts they were learning. There was a clear purpose for learning. The activities students were doing in the classroom were aligned with the standards and focused on applying knowledge and problem solving. Focusing on complex responses and having students actively experience concepts is validated by research.

Secondly, some of the instructional strategies teachers employed helped scaffold student learning. A variety of instructional strategies helps with the gradual release of responsibility for learning. Scaffolding learning is best practice and involves the use of graphic organizers, collaborative student work and formative assessments before independent practice. The use of instructional strategies helps move us away from assigning activities to *teaching* students to think at deeper levels.

Thirdly, it was great to see anchor charts and rubrics posted in classrooms. Having varied and original projects displayed along with substantive feedback is right on target with best practice. It's difficult to get better at something without feedback. Finally, the observed co-teaching model was seamless. Aligned with best practice,

195

the co-teaching team worked in concert to help all students learn. To the observer, it was difficult to determine who the general education teacher was and who the special education teacher was. That is the beauty of the co-teaching model when it is functioning as designed.

I would like to highlight several classrooms that exemplified student engagement in meaningful tasks as well as higher order skills.

- In a science classroom, students were engaged in inquiry. The "Big Idea" was written on the board. Students were engaged in rich discussion related to the concept. Students were constructing knowledge and understanding through collaboration and discussion related to the topic. What was great about this discussion it was student led. Students were posing questions like, "I support Jenny's hypothesis regarding . . . but I wonder . . ."

- In an English classroom, students were writing original ballads. They were able to share the critical components of a ballad and what made a ballad effective. They had studied ballads and had models to draw on for comparison and for exemplars. They were collaborating with peers when needed. The room had a writer's workshop atmosphere with the teacher as facilitator.

- In a social studies classroom, students were studying popular culture and poverty. The teacher used "pair-share" as a strategy to engage all learners in the rich discussion. Peer collaboration before large group discussion allows all students the time to solidify their thinking and engages all learners in the discussion.

- In "walking the walls" in a reading classroom, anchor charts and rubrics were posted. Products that were created for real events and audiences were displayed. It is best practice when displaying student work to include the rubrics and expectations. It is also best practice to exhibit varied and original products – not just the exemplary products.

In summary, as we continue to develop lessons for our classes, we need to continue to ask ourselves what the big idea is that we want them to leave class knowing. How might we be explicit in helping students know and understand the lesson's purpose? How might we pose rich questions and give students a chance to share ideas with each other and with us? If we are clear on our purpose for instruction, then we can begin to take steps to move students to doing rich, engaging work. How might we continue to shift more of the work to the student? Take some time in your PLC to discuss this and then try out some of the ideas.

Principal

Focused Walkthrough Feedback

I recently completed the focused walkthrough that set out to answer the question: "Why are students not making the gains that we expect in language arts?" This adventure in inquiry led me to the following conclusion after observing each of you: **your language leads students to do the cognitive work of comprehending text**. Specific and intentional cues and prompts are needed to guide kids to do the thinking while they read. They should be using evidence, drawing conclusions, and summarizing. The conference is an opportunity to talk with students about their conclusions, and lead them to discuss the author's ideas around language, structure, and purpose. The following questions can help structure the conversations with students during your conferences.

- Why did the author use this choice of words to help you draw that conclusion?
- How does the point of view within affect our understanding of a theme?
- How does the author's choice of words illustrate the mood of the article?
- How does the author evoke emotion within a reader?
- What words and phrases does the author use to demonstrate motivation?

In looking at student work, students are able to identify the author's purpose, but are not necessarily aware of the language that does that and how it explicitly impacts the meaning. However, when conferring in one-to-one or small group settings, we can build off of what kids do know and provide just enough scaffold to help them bridge the gap. I clearly saw this occurring in one of your classrooms. The student was working to respond to a piece of text that he read and was citing evidence or reasons to support his conclusion. The teacher had identified the misconception but guided the student's thinking through statements like, "What language did you use to support your reason?" and "This is the specific quote you took from the text; tell me about this." She also was very specific in how she reinforced the child's thinking by reading his words and saying, "I can tell that this is your thinking that is supported by that piece of text." Throughout the conference the teacher used the language of the standard which modeled for the child; by the conclusion of their discussion the student was also using this academic vocabulary to support his thinking.

It is important to remember that gaining an understanding of how important it is to intentionally scaffold works to BUILD and support the child's thinking. We are continuing to refine and clarify our language and purpose through questioning. Taking the time to plan, rehearse, and reflect on those we write together during our PLC will benefit our work together and ultimately raise achievement.

Your strength is the intentional language that you use; be concise and to the point.

Achievement flows where your intention goes.

Implementation Study Feedback

Implementation Study: Guided Instruction

Look For: Teacher use of prompts, cues, questions are focused and intentional with regard to moving thinking or GLE. In reviewing the charts any component that indicates 80% fidelity would be cause for celebration. Those that are less than 80% would be used as areas for improvement through professional development.

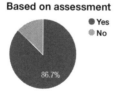

Based on assessment

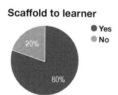

Scaffold to learner

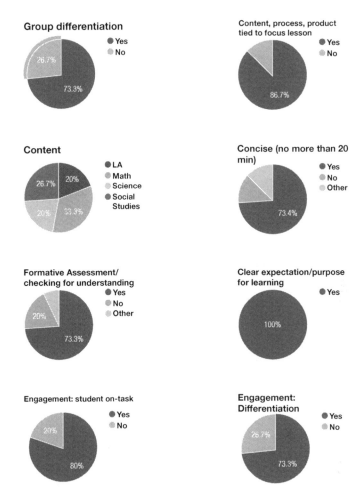

Supervisory Feedback Letter

Individual commitment to a group effort—that is what makes a team work, a company work, a society work, a civilization work.

Vince Lombardi

It's so appropriate that I write the blog about last week's walkthrough on Superbowl Sunday because the two teams who arrive to this game are the year's exemplars of teamwork. It is a process of working together to achieve a goal. Your work and effort was clearly visible throughout the building. It is evident that our school is flying in formation as a team. Specifically, evidence of learning team, collaborative planning and collegial support were in every classroom we visited.

Consider the following statements from our look for document:

- I can utilize the **workshop model**.
- I can **collaborate** in **learning teams**.
- I can use the **curriculum** to **plan** and differentiate, meaningful tasks.
- **Student work displays** will have a clearly posted focus, **rubric**, and student and/or **teacher comments**.
- Teachers will confer and give written and/or oral **feedback** based on **rubrics**.

It is exciting to see these elements in your classrooms. You've demonstrated that executing our SIP plan is making a difference. You are realizing the impact you are having on student achievement and the influence you have on reading/writing behavior. The focus on the curriculum, quality of task, and monitoring through assessment will be the difference in the achievement at our school.

Teachers and teams are flying in formation. We saw 100% compliance with student work display. On each **display** teachers had posted **feedback** that was directly aligned to the work posted. Teachers cited specific evidence from the work and tied it to the grade level expectation of the unit. For example, we saw five social studies displays that student feedback specifically mentioned citing evidence from the text to support concepts like the role of Thomas Jefferson in US history. In sixth grade both displays indicated high level of integration of language arts standard in their display. The work display gave strong indication that students were getting a double dose of reading and writing. Their feedback directly related to the **rubric** posted and content that students were expected to learn. Next steps will be for you to focus on the learning target and lifting the depth of knowledge or expectation on Bloom's taxonomy. Ask students to analyze, synthesize, or evaluate. It is the next step. Challenge yourself and your students with higher expectations for thinking and display that in your classrooms. Make sure your feedback is specifically tied to the learning target. Consider using a question to lift their practice through reflection.

Level	Key Words
Analysis	compare/contrast, deconstruct, infer, discriminate
Synthesis	categorize, compile, compose, rearrange, summarize, modify
Evaluation	appraise, conclude, critique, interpret, relate, evaluate, describe, explain

Evidence of **collaboration** in **learning teams** was another highlight. The **learning team** structure asks teachers to backward plan using the **curriculum** and **planning** instruction accordingly. These elements are critical first steps; but without formative assessment and implementation it would be unlikely it would be observed. Simply stated: You planned, assessed and implemented. We saw this in your classroom providing clear evidence of your work with your learning team. Dr. Mausbach and I observed elements of the **workshop model** in various stages, again 100% in formation. The collaborative effort was obvious in the four language arts classrooms that were working on close reading and citing evidence. They specifically referenced skills from the standards during guided practice by asking students to use a shared text to write support for an inference. Their intentional language sounded like *"Can you take us back to the text?"* and *"Point to the line or work that supports your thinking."* When the students couldn't complete the prompt the teacher immediately went into a think-aloud demonstrating the strategy. Similar statements of purpose were heard in all four classrooms. **Collaboration** in action. Basically when your students understand the purpose of the lesson, they learn more and achieve higher. Next steps will be to state your purpose clearly and then ask students for clarification or application.

Schools that fly high are much like a flock of birds, they fly farther and faster because of their tightly knit collaboration and ability to keep focused on a distant goal.

Prompt for response: Our eye is on a target that we intend to reach: higher achievement. All of us need to take turns supporting each other as we fly. What is your role in the formation? What evidence are you collecting and how will you know you've done your part?

APPENDIX

Thought for the Week Examples

Example A: All Great Leaders are Part Irish

I am fortunate enough to be *almost* 100% Irish (which means I am really about 75%). On days like today I tend to round up when it comes to my heritage but my grandmother, Pearl O'Neill Marron, was the real deal. Grandma Marron evokes many memories about Irish traits and traditions, but one memory that has stuck with me the most centers around her death. Grandma Marron believed, like many true Irish people of her generation, that if her body was not watched after the wake until the next morning when it was officially laid to rest, banshees (evil spirits) would take her soul and she would not be able to rest in peace. I remember my mom and her siblings taking shifts through the night so that Grandma's soul was in safe keeping.

You must be as vigilant in your school improvement efforts as the Irish mourner. If you don't watch over the improvement plan all sorts of forces transpire to get the school off course. There are a myriad of evil forces that can get in the way of our intense focus. These include, but are not limited to: angry parents, discipline issues, allowing management items to consume time, adopting something because the school/district next door is doing it . . . evil spirits everywhere.

The only way to put these spirits to rest is for you to have a laser-like commitment to your clearly defined path for school improvement. This means that all of your resources are pointed in one direction so both short- and long-term goals can be accomplished. The school's mission aligns with the improvement plan, professional development plan and supervision efforts. You are carefully collecting data that will help you make decisions about whether the plan is working or what needs to be adjusted. The leader is watching, continually watching.

There are many more things we can learn from the Irish, but for today lead like a good Irishman and be vigilant.

Happy St. Patrick's Day!

Example B: Leadership Lessons from the Chilean Miners

I am mesmerized by the miners in Chile and their plight. The videos of their rescue have overwhelmed me with feelings of joy, hope, and a belief that the good guys do win. As I reflect on the drama that has unfolded before us I think there are many lessons we can take away from this experience that may just make us stronger leaders.

Lesson 1: Never Give Up

While I am sure the miners had their moments over the course of two months it was evident that they never gave up. They all believed they would survive. Staying the course and believing in the work you are doing can be a terrifically daunting task when you are faced with overwhelmed teachers, disgruntled parents, and students that make poor choices. The mark of a good leader is one who never gives up, who perseveres, even in the toughest of times.

Lesson 2: The Right Tools Matter

From the drill that created the shaft to the capsule that eventually pulled the miners out, the tools made the difference. The tools had to be precise and each had a specific function to perform that aided in the overall success of the rescue mission. Remember your tools and use them appropriately as you try to change your school. Your tools are the data consult, your SIP and PD plan, walkthroughs, and supervision conference skills. All of these tools working together are critical to your successful mission—improved teaching and learning.

Lesson 3: When Making a Big Change, Be Prepared

The rescue attempt started long before the men were put in the capsule. Attention was paid to many important details such as their diet and protective clothing. Once out of the capsule the team on the ground made sure medical services were available to meet immediate and long-term needs (the miners will receive six months of psychological counseling). As you prepare to implement major changes in your school you have to be cognizant of what your staff need prior to and during the change. Our work with Motion Leadership will help us make the big changes.

Lesson 4: Surround Yourself with a Highly Qualified Team

It took the work of many, highly skilled, highly qualified individuals to get the miners to safety. I have found it fascinating that not one person has been the face of the rescue efforts, but many faces. Complex work requires a team of highly committed individuals. Surround yourself with the best team you can and empower them to help you move your school forward. You cannot do it alone.

Lesson 5: Hope Helps

There is a saying, "Hope is not a plan." He is right, but hope can move normal people to do great things. The definition of hope is the desire with expectation of obtainment, or to expect with confidence. Hope leads us to belief. The miners and their rescuers believed they would be successful. They had hope. The absence of hope leads to despair and despair to lack of action. We have to have hope that we will make a difference in the lives of the students in our care. As tough as some days can be in this work, do not lose hope.

Rescuing miners or rescuing children—they both require great leaders. What do you think?

Data Analysis Guide

Data Analysis Guide
2013–14 Data
Planning for 2014–15

People without information cannot act. People with information cannot help but act.

Ken Blanchard

The following tasks/questions are intended as *a guide* for analyzing your data. **USE THESE QUESTIONS TO HELP GUIDE YOUR PREPARATION FOR THE DATA CONSULT.**

Demographics

● Review mobility and free and reduced lunch data. Has the demographics of your school changed significantly over time?

● Review the number of special education referrals, placements, and percentage of students placed. What data is used to determine student referrals? How does your building data look in relation to other schools, district?

● What percent of your student population qualifies for English language learner services? How has this changed over time?

● What percent of your student population qualifies for talented and gifted services? How has this changed over time?

High School Only

● What is your graduation rate and dropout figures for the last five years? Are numbers increasing?